MAINLINE

D1193380

by

HONORABLE GEORGE W. MALONE
United States Senator from Nevada

The LONG HOUSE, Inc.

1958

The L O N G H O U S E, Inc.
PUBLISHERS

POST OFFICE BOX 3
NEW CANAAN — CONN.

CONTENTS

APPENDIX

GEORGE WILSON MALONE

Hon. George W. Malone

United States Senator from Nevada

Senator Malone's office in Washington is a small museum of Western Americana. Etchings of the high plateaux of his native State cover the walls; saddles, throw-ropes, highly polished pine-cones and Navajo artwork surround the visitor. The atmosphere is authentic; the Senator grew up in the saddle.

During his senior year at the University of Nevada he was captain of the baseball and football teams. That was in 1917. When war was declared he volunteered, rose to sergeant in the 40th Division Field Artillery in France, and was subsequently Lieutenant, line officer and regimental intelligence officer. He was the middleweight boxing champion of the Division in 1918. When the war was over, he returned to Reno and re-entered the University of Nevada as an engineering student. In 1920 he won the middleweight championship of the Pacific Coast for his University.

In 1928 Malone organized the Nevada Council of the Boy Scouts of America and became successively its president, the regional director of the Pacific District, and a member of the National Executive Board. During these years he was also a Departmental commander and a National Vice Commander of the American Legion. He is a member of the Veterans of Foreign Wars.

In 1946 George Malone was elected to the Senate of the United States. He is the only practicing professional engineer to be so honored by the people of a sovereign State.

Senator-elect Malone came to the Upper House with a background of competence and experience. He was a consultant on the Shasta and the San Joaquin Dams, and on the Central Valley, Los Angeles and Orange County Flood Control projects in California. He had been Nevada's State Engineer from 1927 to 1935, and president of the Nevada State Board of Registered Professional Engineers and of the Association of Western State Engineers. He was a member of the Public Service and Colorado River Commissions during the legislative action which authorized the building of the Hoover Dam, and during its construction. He was adviser on the generation of power to the Secretary of the Interior during the first administration of Franklin Roosevelt, resigning in 1935.

From 1937 to 1944 Malone served as managing director and editor of the Industrial West Foundation, which published a 3,000-page volume entitled *Western Economic Empire.* This volume set forth exhaustively the potential resources, and their development, of eleven western States, Alaska, Hawaii and the Philippine Islands.

With the outbreak of another world war, Malone divided his time between the West and Washington. From 1942 to 1945 he was special consultant on strategic and critical materials to the Senate Military Affairs Committee and to the Secretary of War during Roosevelt's third and fourth terms as President. He was sent on highly confidential missions to Alaska and into the combat areas of the Southwest Pacific. Danger was something he took in stride with all the others, as the men who saw and knew him there will attest.

When this war ended, a new era of peace and cooperation was envisioned. Malone attended the sessions in San Francisco which formally set up the United Nations Organization, having been appointed its observer by the Senate Military Affairs Committee.

This, in briefest form, was the complex background which George Malone brought to Washington when he took his seat as Nevada's junior Senator at the convening of the first session of the Eightieth Congress in January of 1947.

He at once plunged into a study of the actual, and the potential, strategic situation of the Nation.

During adjournments, he spent his own time and money in purposeful travel abroad. The first year he was a Senator he visited every one of the Marshall Plan countries, and in the Middle East he inspected the petroleum-producing areas of Iraq and Iran. The next year he went to the Far East, the Malay States, Indo-China and Africa. He went to South America in 1949 and again in 1954. He went to Central America in 1950. In 1955 he toured the Balkan countries and spent more than two months in the U.S.S.R.

Wherever he went, in whatever country he visited, Senator Malone applied himself to the purpose of his visit with the mind of a trained engineer. Two things were uppermost in his thoughts. They were these:

What was the relationship between facts and events as he saw them, and the strategic position of these United States; and

What was the cumulative effect of other countries' policies upon the workingmen and investors of his own Nation, whether in industry or on ranch or farm?

He reported his findings to his colleagues in the Senate, in floor debates; the committees on which he served published literally thousands of pages of his reports. The people of Nevada reelected him to the Senate in 1952.

For the next two years Senator Malone was chairman of the Minerals, Materials and Fuels Economics Subcommittee of the Senate Committee on Interior and Insular Affairs. He now is ranking minority member of the latter Committee and a member of the Senate Committee on Finance.

This is the man whose reports and analyses you are about to read, and whose specific proposals are presented for your assessment.

THE PUBLISHERS

PART I

CONTROVERSY

For five generations, *controversy* was the very intellectual lifeblood of our Nation. No great issue faced our people—not a one—but which had its advocates, and its opponents. Editors, writers, journalists, men in public affairs, citizens; all freely expressed their views. They pulled no punches. They said what they meant, and they meant what they said. People read and listened to arguments on both sides and finally, in their wisdom, the people decided the matter.

A change has somehow been brought about in such procedure. A great many of us would like to see once more the discussion of issues, the even violent give-and-take of public debate. I am one of them.

I do not believe that matters of public concern should be soft-pedaled because they are proclaimed to be "controversial".

And this book will be controversial.

A Movement —— in Form, a Pincers

I shall present certain public matters which directly concern every citizen in the forty-eight States. The matters to which I refer affect our industries, our agriculture, our standard of living, our employment. And I am going to present those matters, together with my views and my reasons for holding them.

The thesis which I present is that a pincers movement is now in operation both on the domestic and on the international scene, and that evidence shows that this movement bodes no good for us. The evidence is at times clear. Often it is so subtle as to require considerable application to be unearthed. The first jaw of the pincers is political; the second is economic.

A clear and present illustration of the political jaw is the Status of Forces Agreement, a part of the NATO Pact. This agreement puts the personnel of America's Armed Forces, *and the civilian component,* under the jurisdiction of foreign courts and law. Unless that jurisdiction is waived by the country concerned, any such American who is charged with an offense against the laws of the country in which he is stationed, has no recourse to a single guarantee of the very Nation whose citizen he is, and at whose orders he is stationed abroad. The effective rights of his citizenship—his rights to protection according to American practices of civil and criminal justice—have been surrendered. And while the situation is at present confined to military personnel and the civilian component, who shall say when the theory of its application will not be broadened? Who shall say when, or under what circumstances, *every* American will not be included in its terms? Under this theory, who can say what times, what circumstances, even what single event, will not place under foreign jurisdiction the men who man our ships; the officers who run them; the owners who operate them—when either or all are found within foreign jurisdictional waters, or ports, or ashore? Who shall say that the executives and key personnel of American plants overseas will not, together with their families, similarly be included in its terms? Who can deny the possibilities, now that the principle has been established?

These are typical of the questions which may legitimately be raised as one feels the pressure of one of the jaws of the pincers—the political jaw.

The pressure of the economic jaw is not so clearly felt. Those affected by it are in business; they live in widely scattered parts of our Country. Their single hurt and protests have seemed personal, confined to profit, and unrelated to the national interest; and these protests have been described, therefore, as basely commercial and (apparently) as removed from the greater interests of humanity. Yet the single pressures, the hurt to individuals and to widely separated enterprises, is a thing which accumulates. And as it accumulates it is hurting all of us. It is causing spotted unemployment, the closing of plants. It is causing some firms to transfer their bases, and others to open plants abroad—from which latter goods are being shipped to our own great market. However imperceptibly, this is adding to unemployment. The economic pressure has been growing, quietly and steadily.

There has been, and is, organized denial that such pressure exists. And those upon whom the pressure is applied have, as I say, been scattered, and not organized. Now others are commencing to feel the impact of policies whose purposes have been very differently set forth. They are finding to their sorrow (and often to their surprise) that early predictions of their ultimate effect were exaggerated not at all. More and more of our citizens have been devoting time and study to the situation.

Few there are who have noted the *dual* impact of its political and economic jaws. Yet pincers it is. The two jaws are there—and the one without the other would be a fulcrum only.

The Beginning

The pincers are covered; its jaws have teeth. Both jaws are wrapped in velvet most attractive. On the political side, the velvet is embossed with words which are carefully selected. They include such phrases as "the freedom-loving world", "the Western allies", "international cooperation", "collective security", and "defence against aggression".

The economic jaw also is wrapped in velvet layers, the foremost of which bears two words: "World Trade". Underneath these two words there gradually appeared a third. This word is "Reciprocity". It is embossed in gold.

At first, this word did not appear at all. It then could occasionally be seen, if you looked closely, and its lettering was very fine. Gradually the letters seemed larger, and they were. The enlargement gave rise to the thought, with some, that the word had been there all the time; that the boldface only appeared as first one light velvet layer was removed, and then another. This, indeed, is the way it was.

Here was the slogan of "world trade" in one fine word—"reciprocity". This word neglected certain facts, some of which concerned tariffs.

The history of tariffs—taxes levied upon imported goods—needs but brief review. Authority for such levies was explicit in our Constitution; it was vested in the legislative branch. At that time, the end of the eighteenth century, two schools of thought existed in the world of trade. Some people advocated "free trade", others favored "protection". Britain—whose economy rested on the import of cheap raw materials, duty-free, and the export of manufactured goods—was the prime example of "free trade". Britain's theory and practice did not change until early in the present century. Both grew directly out of the Industrial Revolution, as did the economy upon which they were based.

The situation in the young American Republic was immediately different. Following our War of Independence, British traders quite naturally rushed to flood the new-world market with their products. The ex-Colonials had practically no industry. And there, in a nutshell, was the problem. The two schools of thought clashed head-on. They debated the issue, openly, thoroughly, and free-for-all. The Congress voted to protect the new Nation's "infant industries". Duties upon imports were imposed, and in the year 1791 the average impost was 15.34 percent. Whatever the subsequent arguments, our infant industries grew. "Protection" was by no means the sole factor which brought about this growth, not at all. But it was *one* of the factors, and an important one.

Shortly after this policy was adopted—only twenty years—our people and Nation faced the War of 1812. And now an added factor entered the minds of cautious men. The factor was *defense*. The young Nation came through this second war still in possession of its independence, but a lesson had been learned. And it was strict. It was this: That no nation may properly sacrifice its capacity for *defense* production—even in return for "trade". It was the realization of this principle that convinced Thomas Jefferson—until then a warm advocate of free trade—that a system of import duties was essential to the wellbeing of the Nation.

Import duties were increased. From 13.07% in 1812 they were raised to averages of 24% during the decade 1811-20, and to 37.37% in the ten-year period following. It then became practical to lower the average duties to 31.22%, 27.01% and 24.06% during the next three decades. The figures are in no way cited to "annoy" you; they are given to illustrate concretely the second factor of protection, *i.e.,* legitimate national defense.

The theory of protection brought an all-time high in import duties between the years 1891 and 1900. The average reached 46.73% during that decade. It then declined. Between 1913 and 1920 the average was lowered at an almost uniform rate of 3 percent per year, to 16.4%. Then it rose.

And did import rates apply only to those commodities which were in competition with manufactured products? Were they solely for the advantage of "industry"? No. In 1920, three new forces entered the picture. They were these: Foreign producers began dumping onto the American markets *agricultural* products—below the foreign cost of production; their governments began to engage in widespread devaluation of their currencies, and for the purpose of negating the duties imposed by others upon their products; and thirdly, the farmers of America demanded in no uncertain terms that they be protected against such practices. The Emergency Tariff Act of 1921 was rushed into law. Wheat, flaxseed, corn, beans, peanuts, potatoes, rice, onions; peanut, cottonseed and soya bean oil; cattle, sheep, and fresh and frozen meats; cotton, wool, sugar, butter, cheese, milk, tobacco, apples, cherries—all these products of ranch and farm were protected, and many more.

Then came the Tariff Act of 1922. A new concept was introduced, and this was the concept of "flexibility". The President was authorized by Congress to increase, or to reduce, existing rates by not more than 50 percent, *after thorough investigation by the Tariff Commission*. This Commission had been created in 1916 as an agency of the Congress. Few changes were made by a President pursuant to the Act of 1922, and the changes usually were to increase a levy. The concept, therefore, might be called "flexible protection". Congress remained the governing body, as designed by the Constitution.

This situation prevailed from 1922 until the year 1934.

The year 1934 saw a complete change in theory. It was the year to which may be traced the first concrete evidence that there was a pincers, and that it had jaws. And in 1934 there was wrapped around the economic jaw the first bolts of that soft velvet which ever since has so gently encased its teeth.

The means employed were legislative. The instrument was the Congress. And the 1934 legislation which the Congress passed was the Trade Agreements Act.

For the urgency of this legislation the executive chose the Department of State. At the head of this Department was a Southern gentleman. He it was who, years before—in the House of Representatives—had sponsored the bill which ultimately was to place in our Constitution the Sixteenth Amendment; the gentleman who, when that bill was being debated in the House, guided it to its final passage, and argued *against* a 10 percent limitation on the proposed income tax because—be it noted—a 10 percent maximum would itself become the minimum! In 1934 this man was Secretary of State. His name was Cordell Hull. He presented to the Nation the Trade Agreements Act.

The economic jaw of a pincers had been forged. This Act was its first fine wrapping.

It was the beginning.

1934. The Trade Agreements Act

The moment was propitious. Trade was at an unbearable minimum all over the globe. People everywhere were in despair; in places, they were desperate. Leadership was wanted—leadership out of the depression; leadership to take 10,000,000 and more Americans from the despair of unemployment and put them once more to work, creative if possible, otherwise if it were not.

Washington provided that leadership.

Out of Washington came programs by the score, political and economic. The national Congress approved them, and those who so voted were reelected by their constituents—for good or ill. And if—as there were—some in office did discern in these programs what looked like hidden teeth; if—as there were—others not in office rose to point out dangers, a sick Nation did not pause to examine too seriously the prescriptions handed out by experts.

Did these prescriptions, any or all of them, combine to cure the ailments; or did they but alleviate for a time the symptoms? Did they, on the political scene, bring surcease from war and fear of war—even at the price of ultimately subjecting Americans to foreign law—or did they eventually commit our youth and Nation to *every* war, be it small or large? Did they, on the economic scene, bring "peace through trade"— even at the sacrifice of an adjustable modicum of our home market; or are they progressively sacrificing that market, and the earning standards to which our citizens are accustomed—in return for neither peace, nor mutually profitable trade?

Let us examine the Trade Agreements Act, and find some facts. Let us then examine what has followed upon that Act and find, if we can, the actual results of its "reciprocity". Then, in the light of results and determined fact, let us submit the entire theory to examination.

The appeal upon which the 1934 Act was to be based, is a matter of public record. The Democratic platform of 1932 voiced it, and it sounded well. The platform read:

> We advocate a competitive tariff for revenue, with a fact-finding Tariff Commission free from Executive interference, reciprocal trade agreements with other nations, and an international economic conference designed to restore international trade and facilitate exchange.

> We condemn the Hawley-Smoot tariff law, the prohibitive rates of which have resulted in retaliatory action by more than 40 countries, created international economic hostilities, destroyed international trade, driven our factories into foreign countries, robbed the American farmer of his foreign markets, and increased the cost of production.

A national administration was elected, to remain in office for twenty years.

And now, before I go any further, let me say this: I am a Republican. The administration elected to office in 1932 was Democratic. Twenty years' development of the theory inherent in its trade and tariff platform was under Democrat administrations. The results, as I see them, are not to be viewed with political partisanship. I do not speak of them as a Republican. I view the results in the only way I know—what I believe to be best for our people and Nation, and I believe this statement will be confirmed. When the Republican Party was returned to office in 1952, the identical theory was pursued, and identical results further accrued. There was no discernable change. Indeed, steps even more drastic were taken, and these steps followed the exact pattern which had been established under the 1934 Act. Under its velvet covering, the economic pincers continued to press; under its velvet covering, the political jaw continued to press. The Status of Forces Agreement was endorsed, and driven through to enactment, by the Republican command. The pincers movement became openly a bipartisan affair.

The 1932 platform was implemented by the Trade Agreements Act in 1934. And the following is an extremely brief summary of the platform-claims, and of how they were carried out in fact:

1. The "competitive tariff for revenue" became a tariff which was not competitive at all; and it became a tariff whose revenue was year after year progressively less;

2. The Tariff Commission which was to be "free from Executive interference"—and which under the 1930 flexible tariff Act was responsible directly to Congress—became a body which was dominated by, and was completely subservient to, the Executive branch;

3. The "reciprocal" agreements developed into contracts whose terms were totally negated by restrictions imposed by other nations, while by their terms our Country continued to open its markets to the goods which these others produced. The word "reciprocity" was nowhere written in the Act;

4. Conferences designed to "restore" international trade became conferences at which such trade was "restored" by give-away programs financed by the taxpayers of these United States, and by moves which further opened the *American* market to others' wares;

5. Exchange was "facilitated" by the imposition, by other nations, of the greatest and most diversified restrictions upon *our* goods that the world of commerce had ever seen;

6. The "retaliatory action" for which the Smoot-Hawley tariff was blamed, became itself vastly multiplied in scope, and demonstrably designed to evade and negate every *quid pro quo* which the trade agreements were publicly asserted to contain;

7. The "economic hostilities" which the Act was claimed to palliate, became a sustained and all but invisible cold war;

8. The international trade which had been "destroyed" by the former tariff not only was not restored (outside of the war traffic and give-away programs which, you will agree, are hardly legitimate trade), it dwindled year by year, as the figures show;

9. The Act was to remove the causes which had "driven our factories into foreign countries"; and the Act, and its succeeding agencies and commitments, proceeded to create conditions which *encouraged* American factories to move abroad and in the process to progressively lessen their employment of men and women here;

10. The tariff, it was claimed, had "robbed the American farmer of his foreign markets". Where—after more than twenty years—are those markets now?

11. The question as to whether the tariff had "increased the cost of production" is too complex for proper evaluation here. Let me say this, however: So long as the policies of this Government are permitted to remain such as can only be sustained by managed money and inflation, just so long will the American "cost of production" increase. The very *theory* of the Trade Agreements Act, together with its succeeding agencies and involvements, is inflationary *per se*.

These points summarize what actually took place, in contrast to the trade program which was publicly set forth in the platform of 1932. When twenty years later another administration was voted into office, the identical theory was followed, in an identical way. The effect upon the Nation will be shown to be identical, and the pressures will be seen as cumulative.

Politically, the jaw of the pincers has increasingly revealed its teeth. The claims of its early opponents, that the ultimate purpose was world government, have not diminished. On the contrary, the conviction has increased, as has the evidence adduced in its support.

Economically, the pincers' jaw has been more gently, more subtly, felt. Yet it is there. And if this theory is not changed, the agencies and policies which it embraces will—inevitably—jockey our Republic into a position of strategic weakness, if not of total dependence. We will have forgotten the lesson so hardly learned from the War of 1812. Even our Nation's defense will depend upon the "cooperation" of turbulent political authorities far removed from our ideological or geographical shores.

What might fail by political means could thus, all unseen by us, be accomplished by means which are economic.

We can escape from the political jaw by a reversal of our foreign policy. We cannot escape from the economic jaw until we discover what it is and how it works, and then in cold but friendly approach adopt another theory, one which will, in effect, say this: We want what is good for *our* people and Nation; you want what is good for your own. And this is right and proper. Where no *mutual* advantage is to be found, we will find no basis of sustained agreement; where our interests *are* found as mutual, we have the true basis for give-and-take. Let us sit down together and talk it over.

This theory works at home; it works with neighbors; it works in business. There is no reason on God's green earth it cannot work with nations. It is true reciprocity. And it is true leadership. It commands respect.

The Wearers of the Purple

From the time of our War of Independence, through the War of 1812 and to the present day, there have been two broad ideas of government in the world. Our own was new; the other, old.

A startling transfer of sovereignty—from the head of state to the people—was basic to our Constitution. It released forces hitherto unknown. Possession of ultimate sovereignty by a people, for the first time in history now governing themselves, freed the minds of men for unlimited activity in every field. And were I asked what I thought was the single key force behind America's vast success, I would say that it was this one, for it unlocked forever the doors of the individual human mind. Out of that mind came myriad ideas, and from the sum total of those ideas grew the vast and prosperous continent whose boundaries encased the happy Republic.

To Congress was entrusted its protection. And the Congress, in its wisdom, kept trade free within the States and established such duties upon imports as were felt would contribute to the sound development of all sections of the Country alike. The economic result was to be a tremendous and unprecedented market, continental in its breadth and scope.

Politically, older countries with few exceptions clung to their own institutions and beliefs. Switzerland modelled her constitution after our own; the republics of South America took from it their several inspirations. But, after six generations of amazingly successful example, there have been no serious emulations of our unique political structure—or of our theory of government—abroad. And that is right and proper; other peoples live there, not we.

Economically, each country has sought for itself the greatest export trade which it could develop. Clearly, the world's greatest single market is our own. I can hold no brief against others for the efforts they make to capture that market; it is a natural thing to do. Their practices—due to their political and social structures—are, to be sure, not those of individual enterprise. Their combinations vary from leagues and guilds and cartels, to monopolies of the state. The political authorities, the governments, are always present, and to a degree unknown in America until very recent years. The politico-economic structure abroad is such that the political authority—the government—must be understood by Americans to be an integral part of foreign trade, and accepted as such. To know and understand this factor is essential to any realistic assessment of "world trade", certainly in the contemplation of a theory upon which world trade properly can be based.

It was this combination—not individual businessmen—which immediately attempted to recapture the American market at the end of our War of Independence, and which resulted in our adoption of the "protective" tariff. It was the same combination which resulted in our recognizing the factor of national defense, following the War of 1812. It was against this combination that the American tariff system was erected. The system was flexible, and the flexibility itself made possible the periodic adjustments whose purpose was the achievement of fair and reasonable competition and the elimination of the system's recurrent inequities. And, for all its admitted drawbacks, the system contributed in large measure to the highest standard of earned rewards ever enjoyed by any people in the history of the world.

Whether by intent or progressively by accident, the Trade Agreements Act of 1934 abandoned this American system and adopted the politico-economic theory which was traditional abroad. The business and the enterprise of individuals now were considered in close connection with the policies of the state. The state would assist them in the expansion of their markets. Government itself would negotiate the channels of trade, and, in the slough of despond which in those depression years was so widespread, few there were who would decline apparent alleviation; even fewer discerned in the program the entering wedge of state control.

The channels of trade were opened—but by definition. Goods and wares were shipped—but by treaties which were permissive. The Nation breathed for a time a little freely, for were not governments—all governments—now meeting together for a purpose? And was not this purpose to "free world trade"?

There was no clear reason for people to think of these meetings in terms of the theory of government itself. But when the governments met, they had at their base two broad and distinct ideas. Of the two, our own was new; the other had not changed since history began. And in these meetings of the political authorities the theory which for five generations had sustained the new, was surrendered. Somewhere in the process had been diminished the recognition of its strength, and the old discarded theory had been reembraced.

The age-old theory was this: The State would determine trade.

Those at high level within the political authority would be the chiefs.

On the American scene there had emerged, from out a distant past, individuals with a mission. They had been long at work in education and in politics, and now they entered business. Their counterparts had for centuries been fawned upon in Europe's courts. All unsuspecting, we Americans had now produced our own.

They became, overnight, the courtiers of The State. In its executive branch they would come to flourish, as the wearers of the noble purple.

The Policy is Coordinated

Back we went. The legislative branch—the Congress—abdicated a prime function which had been delegated to it, and exclusively to it, by the States under the Federal Constitution. It did not "delegate" this function, as some say. There is no authority in the Constitution for any such "delegation". The Seventy-third Congress abdicated. And in the executive branch the wearers of the purple—not one of whom, appointees or tenuremen, had been elected by the citizens of the Republic—took over the power which the Congress abdicated in the 1934 Act.

What had been vested by the people in their body of elected representatives was the sole power over tariffs. The representatives were responsible personally to their fellows, and impersonally via the ballot-box. By their abdication of the tariff power, the two Houses of Congress enabled non-elective personnel and agencies, located in the executive branch, to take over. And this was precisely what the framers of the Constitution had foreseen, and had provided well against. They knew from history to trust *no* executive, and so they bound their new, American executive by the Constitution's chains. Now the chains themselves were handed over. The executive would employ them. They would be used to bind the Congress and the people.

The abdication took place during a time of depression and of despair. It also took place because the sponsors of the legislation proclaimed to Congress, and to the Nation, that the legislation was a fine thing, and that it was "progressive". It "met conditions in a modern world by means which themselves were modern."

The legislation was none of these things. It was not "progressive"; it was not "modern". By the abdication of the power of the (elected representatives of) the people; by the taking of that power by the appointed or career personnel of the executive branch, the procedure was by its very nature the antithesis of "progressive". It was reactionary. The Congress which abdicated, was reactionary. The executive which took over, was reactionary. And—whether the programs which followed are held to be good or bad—*any* transfer, surrender or abdication of power, to *any* executive branch of government, is the placement of power in the hands of those who are not responsible to a people who are sovereign.

The step was a reversion to the age-old theory of the supremacy of The State. By this procedure, our people have been allowing their individual and sovereign liberty to pass from them—to be exercised for good or ill, but to be exercised *on their behalf* by those over whom they have no observable control. The result is a progressive power-transfer whose very essence is reactionary.

That the procedure is called "progressivism" matters not at all.

So the executive took over, and commenced to put into effect those programs which had been described as designed for "expanding foreign markets for the products of the United States."

To those who, like myself, were watching events with some concern, a number of phenomena shortly became visible. To those who were watching, there appeared other programs, other agencies, other branches of the executive, which seemed to be not unallied to the procedures which followed upon the Act of 1934. There seemed also to be an ever increasing atmosphere of reticence, on the part of the executive, to informing Members of Congress of what was being done—presumably on behalf of them and of the people whom they were elected to represent.

Some of us voiced the thought that these phenomena might in some way be interrelated. Our suggestions were denied. They were denied by the very executive which even then was deeply engaged in such coordination. A vast machine of "news-releases" was built up, and the non-elected personnel of the executive structure were quick to the point of eagerness to state in such releases that those of us who voiced misgivings were at best misinformed; at worst, we were "obstructionists", "enemies of the common man", "opponents of freedom and progress", and certainly we were (*horribile dictu*) "isolationists".

Yet those first cautious ones persisted, and as the years went by their numbers increased. Also, as the years went by, evidence that their concern had not been misplaced was bit by bit accumulating. The concern had two vital aspects. The one was that a coordinated program did exist, and that it boded no good either for our people or for our Nation; the other was that there was building, in our midst, a very good facsimile of the reactionary, centralized state.

In 1949 two events, each minor in itself, did nothing to lessen that concern.

The first occurred during the House Ways and Means Committee hearings on a bill to extend the provisions of the 1934 Trade Agreements Act. An Assistant Secretary of State was testifying. The date was January 24. The Assistant Secretary was Willard L. Thorpe. Mr. Thorpe stated:

(1) The trade-agreements program is an integral part of our over-all program for the world economic recovery.

(2) The European Recovery program (Marshall Plan) extends immediate assistance on a short-time basis to put the European countries back on their feet.

(3) The International Trade Organization, upon which Congress will soon be asked to take favorable action, provides a long-term mechanism by which all countries' commercial policies, in the broadest sense of the term, may be tested and guided into conformity with a pattern which will maximize trade and minimize friction arising out of national trade programs which may be harmful to other countries' legitimate expectations.*

By profession I am an engineer. Engineers' language is clear—to engineers. Doubtless there is a language among officials in the executive branch which is clear and understandable to them, though at times I find difficulty in following it. Nevertheless, I think Mr. Thorpe's statement helped make it quite clear that plan there was, that the plan was a coordinated one, and that it was worldwide.

A second event substantiated in abrupt fashion the thought that there was being erected in our midst—all unknown to the great social

---

*Hearings, p. 7.

body of our people—an operating nucleus of the reactionary, centralized state. The event occurred to me personally.

It did not occur to me as an individual. It happened to me as a duly elected representative of the citizens of a sovereign State. The event embraced the executive's flat denial of information, and information of vital public concern, to a member of the United States Senate. Through him, the people of his State—and through 95 other Senators, the entire citizenry of the Republic—were denied knowledge of what their agency, the Government, was doing in a realm of foreign affairs, presumably for the Nation's good.

The Congress had abdicated. And—though deluged with the claims of benevolent policy on the one hand, and on the other hand denied access to vital information—the people had acquiesced in that abdication. What now took place illustrated, irrefutably, what happens when power is transferred, surrendered or abdicated to the executive of a centralized state. It was a single instance, and it was not a large one. But it was pointed in its implications. It had to do with foreign policy, and with trade.

It came about as a direct result of the fact that for years the subtly vicious suggestion has been heard that matters of public import should not be made *controversial*. The idea has in fact been widely accepted. Here it is illustrated in executive government.

The experience to which I refer took place in March 1949. Some time before, an international conference had met at Annécy, France, and another at Torquay, England. The object of each conference was to "further international trade". One hundred and thirty-three new trade agreements were negotiated. As a Senator, I wanted to know what effect these agreements, and the lowering of tariffs which I presumed they contained, might have upon our own people and Nation.

I wrote to the Department of State. No reply was received. After a more than reasonable wait I asked my administrative assistant to obtain for me a list of the agreements, and copies when possible. My assistant was given a polite brushoff. The executive personnel were very busy, you know; the agreements were scattered, and would not be easy to find. So one morning I picked up the telephone and asked a few pointed questions. The next day 88 of the treaties were brought to my office. As I recall, the emissary of the State Department would leave only 41 or 42 of them with me for study. About a fifth of them were in foreign languages and the copies of these which I was shown had not even been rendered into our own tongue. The remainder of the 88 agreements were so confidential that they could not be left in the possession of a Senator of the United States. Several were so confidential that the man held them in his hands while I looked at them. Understand, these agreements, or treaties, were not made by the United States with other nations. The treaties were between European nations—ECA countries—and countries behind the iron curtain, including the Soviet.

The argument may be advanced that under normal diplomatic procedure these treaties, between foreign nations, were not properly our knowledge. The argument is tenable. Yet a "new era", an era of "cooperation", has been ushered in. Its objectives are "peace", and "world trade". Its theme is "collective security" and "reciprocity". And to set in motion this new era the taxpayers of the United States have for half a generation been picking up the bill. It would seem, at least to me, that the recipients of our funds—those who, we are told, are the beneficiaries, and who therefore love us—would be only too happy to let us know how wisely, how fairly and how "progressively" those funds are being used.

Yet here we have a situation: Our people—and I certainly am one of them—are being told that the "new era" program is a success, and that all our funds are helping to "stop aggression". According to the general consensus, to be sure, "aggression" in 1914 meant the Kaiser; in 1939 it meant Hitler; and beginning in 1945 it meant the changing heads of the U.S.S.R. The abandonment of traditional American policy therefore hardly seems to "stop aggression". It appears but to change its *locale* and speed of incidence, each new focal point proving more expensive and more threatening than the last.

The executive personnel who guide this policy tell us with one voice that we are financing other nations "in order to combat aggression"; with another voice they inform Senators who represent you that treaties which have been negotiated by our (purchased) friends are documents which must not be seen.

And in the denial of access to such agreements, there is contradiction. The inference from it may not at once be clear, but it is there. And the inference is that somewhere there is a consistency behind such contradictions, that a plan has been coordinated, and on a global scale.

I think the assertion will not be successfully contravened that the reactionaries in the executive branch—the wearers of the purple—are saying to us one thing and doing to us another.

Let us see.

The Global Pincers Movement — in Theory and in Fact

The tariff policy of a nation—of any nation—has three legitimate functions: The first function is to raise revenue; the second is to protect the economy of its citizens; the third is to ensure the nation's defense.

These functions have been subordinated to a theory. The theory, broadly speaking, is that the varying political structures of the world, and the varying economies of the world, can be molded into one co-ordinated whole. In pursuance of this theory, it is clear that a series of international organizations must be set up. As these are set up and begin to function, it is also clear that the purposes of each must parallel those of all the others. If the theory is to be made to work, there must be an overall directing guidance, and an overall directing plan.

A great many citizens assert that such a plan exists. The assertion is consistently, even vehemently, denied. Who is right? The burden of proof rests with plaintiff. And the proof must rest on evidence such as to remove all peradventure.

A search for evidence reveals instantly one thing. Evidence, if it exists, is not to be found among legislators; it is not to be found among men and women who are elected by the people to perform the functions of representative government. It is to be found, if at all, within that vast realm defined by the word "executive", or "executive branch". Further, it is to be found only by intense search, a search which goes far beyond the "executive" of the American Government; the search must be pursued among another vast array of agencies, commissions and "authorities". These are international.

The reason for this situation has followed upon the application of a theory. It has come about logically, and in the following manner.

Among nations abroad, sovereign power was traditionally vested in governments, *i.e.*, in the political authority, in the executive, in the state. The states could meet, as sovereign entities, and decide what they might wish. The people concerned did not have to be consulted, for they possessed no sovereignty. The state was all-powerful.

This was not true in America. In these United States the *people* were sovereign. The men who represented our Country abroad were responsible, directly or indirectly, to them. If a treaty were involved, the responsibility was indirect (via the Senate); otherwise responsibility was direct (via the whole of Congress).

The theory of molding into one coordinated whole all the varying political structures of the world, and all its varying economies and standards of living, required that a basic segment of the sovereign power of the people of the United States be removed from them and absorbed into the American executive. The structure of government in the United States must be brought into line with older philosophies which elsewhere had not basically altered since time. The American executive must be made uninhibited, and thus able to meet with other executive authorities, with other governments, in order to determine with them what was to be done. The state, in brief, must become in such conferences all-powerful, as states abroad traditionally were. Then such meetings would be truly international—what they determined was what would be.

That was the theory. And if the personnel of the new American executive could be fired with the vision implicit in the theory, all would be well.

The first step was to invest the American executive with the power sufficient to enter into its fulfillment.

This step was taken by the Seventy-third Congress when it passed the Trade Agreements Act in 1934. The Act was explicit. The sovereign power which Congress had abdicated was absorbed by the executive, and thus removed from the people's control. That power is now being increasingly vested in international groups, and removed from our *Nation's* control. It is a sum of power which is beginning observably to affect the life of every citizen among us. This is the essential result of the application of the theory set forth above.

Does it work? Are its results properly beneficial to our people and to the Republic? Do they reasonably fulfill its announced hopes and expectations, and the claims that the theory is of cumulative benefit to the world? Certainly there are structures which have been erected, and they follow a blueprint which may have existed from the start. There are activities and pressures which emanate from the structures, and they can be felt; they can be recognized, and they can be ascertained.

They are in their nature, two: Political, and economic.

This book is devoted almost wholly to the economic application of the theory. Yet, that we not fail to observe the correlation, let me just mention a few political (and social) structures which have been erected in its pursuit. Whether they be considered right or wrong, good or bad, they are fact.

Suppose we begin with the announcement that "the aggressors" would be "quarantined". This announcement was followed by the abrogation of the Neutrality Act, the destroyer deal with Britain, lend-lease, the convoying of foreign ships. We entered the war. We participated in discussions. And out of those discussions came such facts as the International Food Conference at Hot Springs; UNRRA; Dumbarton Oaks; the Bretton Woods Conference which resulted in the International Bank and Fund; the Preparatory Conference for UNESCO; the San Francisco Conference which set up the United Nations; the NATO and SEATO military alliances; the Genocide Convention; the Declaration of Human Rights . . . .

These political and social instruments, and the military instruments which accompanied them, fitted into a pattern, behind which lay the theory. All of them had this in common: Not one was responsible to the elected public servants of this representative Republic. In each of them, the appointees of the executive branch were free to act.

Where, how, and to what extent the executive chose to act with other political authorities, it could. And it did.

For good or ill, our people have since been subjected to court interpretations which rest on "the principles and purposes of the Charter of the United Nations". In simulated invasion by "United Nations troops", nine communities in California, and others in Texas and New York, have been encroached, subjected to martial law, mayors imprisoned, police chiefs jailed, school teachers dragooned and their pupils ordered about (even at bayonet point). It is claimed that these are "exercises", I know. But they have happened; they are fact. Our men and women in the Services abroad, and their civilian component, are subject to foreign law. Nearly 25,000 cases had been recorded by January 1957. Hundreds have been jailed. And if at times punishment has been justified, that is not the point. International law never questioned that jurisdiction rested with the *sending* country, and with its courts. But the long, slow process of juridical evolution, called "international law", has now been set aside— by formal treaty, sponsored by the United States executive. The Senate passed that treaty. And from it has grown a great and rising controversy, on the subject of "treaty law". Constitutional amendments have been proposed, to stop this sort of thing—whether by treaty or by that newly-broadened means by which a Senate-voted treaty is evaded: The executive agreement. The Secretary of State said in 1955 that there were perhaps 10,000 of them. No one knows what they all contain; no one can possibly know. Yet, according to the theory, they are the Law of the Land, and every court in these United States is bound by their provisions; every citizen is bound by what they contain.

It may be that an amendment to the Constitution would effectively end the matter; it may not. But what *will* end the matter is the abandonment of the theory of which such treaties, executive agreements, and world political authorities are the continually increasing results.

As these and other events have occurred, the teeth of the political jaw of the pincers have been pointedly seen. Are there similar teeth, less easily seen, at the same time being bared in the economic jaw? If so, what are they? How have they been bared? What events followed upon the adoption of the Trade Agreements Act of 1934? Was there parallel—demonstrable parallel—between the events on the political (and social) scene, and those on the economic? And if so, was the parallel resultant upon the application of a theory which was identical to both?

Again I submit that there is a test: Does the theory work; and is it right? These questions must be answered, and upon clearly demonstrable facts.

A good place to start is with the Marshall Plan. The Marshall Plan was economic. In a way, the Marshall Plan might be described as an extension of "reciprocity". It was the means employed to bring the countries of Europe once more to the productive point from which they could "reciprocate". It would enable those countries again to make the products which constitute world trade. The Marshall Plan was America's contribution to Europe's peacetime "rehabilitation". The gift-loans had been followed by UNRRA; three and three-quarter billion dollars had gone to Britain in 1946. Now a vast five-year program was announced. It would raise living standards abroad; it would rehabilitate war-torn economies—and it would start once more, and greatly stimulate, "world trade". It would cost $17,000,000,000.

There was no announcement to those who would pay for the program that already, before a penny of its billions arrived overseas, the production level of those countries was actually above the level maintained before the war. In the least of them (excluding Austria and eastern Germany) the ratio was 110 percent, and in the one whose recovery was most advanced the ratio was 138 percent. The sole exception was of course Germany. For Germany there was devised the Morgenthau Plan.

So Marshall Plan funds were progressively appropriated from the American taxpayer and sent abroad. They were sent to "bolster the economies" of countries whose economies already were from 10 to 38 percent above their level of before the war. The funds raised these percentages further still. And the plant and the machinery which went to industrial Europe went there to produce the very type of products which kept our own assembly lines running, and employed our men. And, as industrialists abroad—always in conjunction with the political authority, remember—would be bound to seek the widest possible markets for their to-be-increased production, a plan was clearly needed to meet the situation.

A plan was forthcoming, and almost at once.

The plan embraced no mere relationship between two nations; it was not based even upon a constant receipt of observable funds from the United States, sent directly to the governments concerned. The plan reversed the entire procedure. The funds would become all but invisible. The plan gave direct access to the markets of the U.S.A.

Working hand in hand, as was their tradition, European industrialists and their political authorities proposed a conference. Proceeding upon the power to which it had succeeded, the American executive at once concurred. The conference was held at Havana, in 1949. From this conference emerged a single great idea. An "authority" would be set up. Its scope would be worldwide. All governments would agree to participation in it, and each would have one vote. This consortium of political authorities would be called the International Trade Organization.

The conferees drew up a charter. This charter, upon subsequent examination, failed to impress one either with its clarity or with its principles. There was in evidence no overwhelming modesty on the part of those whose draft it was. One was not impressed that here were men who, burdened with their responsibility, felt that little by little, that piece by piece, a tremendously complex situation might be resolved. Nor could a good-willed citizen of these United States apply himself to its text and find in it hope that the liberty which he so long had had might, however slowly, become gradually and appreciatively enjoyed by others throughout the world.

What he did find was a non-elected executive authority, global in its scope.

This global authority was to legislate away all evil economic. It was to ensure peaceful international cooperation—by solemn covenant. The covenant required 30,000 words.

To be sure, this covenant was to be submitted to participating governments for their approval. It never reached the floors of Congress. The ITO was never formalized, and it never was set up. Because of this, I may seem wasting your time in discussing it at all. I do not believe I am, and I think that you will soon agree. For the ITO *was* proposed, and its charter, therefore, showed intent. And there is another organization, now in actual operation, which directly parallels the ITO and in some ways is even more specific in its aims. We'll take a look at this one shortly.

The ITO was described as "another step in international cooperation". The press releases were widely publicized and they were almost a repetition of those of fifteen years before which promoted the Trade Agreements Act. The program, however, had now become worldwide. And so, to the eleven points set forth on pages 15-6 herein, others could now be added:

12. Members (governments) were enjoined from subsidizing foreign trade, but they were permitted to subsidize foreign trade if their exports were affected by the subsidies of a nonmember;

13. Each of the charter's provisions is a qualified provision; each has a modifying clause. There is also a blanket clause. This clause states that if an import hurts domestic producers "the member shall be free, in respect of such product, and to the extent and for such time as may be necessary to prevent or remedy such injury, to suspend the obligations [of the charter] in whole or in part or to withdraw or modify the concession." Such escape clauses are not much use to us of course for, as you know, whenever the Congress proposes to amend an international agreement the executive immediately states to the Congress that such amendment will hurt "international cooperation"; the executive at the same time floods the Country with press-releases, radio and TV scripts, and even with pronouncements from Cabinet ranks. This procedure, too, is in conformity with the whole theory, and it is why so many of our people have been so consistently, and so grossly, misinformed;

14. The argument was offered that the charter and its escape clauses benefited us as much as it did others. This is not so. With us, the escape clauses only apply to tariffs. The same clauses permit other nations, traditionally operated on a politico-cartel basis, to continue to impose— or even to establish—far more lethal weapons of trade war, weapons which will be illustrated a little later. An example of how escape clauses operate took place at one international conference in the summer of 1947, at Geneva. The United States delegation had been empowered to make tariff concessions up to 50 percent of the duties then prevailing—in return for comparable concessions, particularly in the form of changes in the British system of "imperial preference". The average American tariff was there reduced from 32 percent to 25 percent. In return, 5 percent of the imperial preference rates were eliminated; 70 percent of them remained untouched. (The progressive elimination of "imperial preference" had been one of the asserted benefits to be achieved by our joining the International Bank!);

15. A reading of the ITO charter brings to the student's mind a strong suspicion. Free trade was a concept of the nineteenth century. Britain was then the preeminent trading and creditor nation. Sterling was convertible everywhere, and at stable rates. And Britain, from the very nature of her economy, was a free trade nation. The result of this, and other factors, was a natural and worldwide condition, one which developed according to the *mores* of its nineteenth century day.

The more one studied the ITO the more one came to suspect that its charter was designed to bring back in the twentieth century the conditions of the nineteenth; that it would itself bring into being a world cartel which would determine the channels of trade, would allocate the commodities of trade, and would say who might purchase what from whom. Even more distinct was the feeling that the American market was the one great market which would be opened, free to all;

16. The charter made it abundantly clear that a single entity was to be supreme. That entity was The State. Inherent in the charter of the ITO was an economic authority, itself composed of states. The authority could set up an economic government of the world.

To this supreme development of the tradition of older countries, America, the new, was expected to acquiesce;

17. To those who see in governmental interference a clearcut working of socialist doctrine, the charter of the ITO was alarming in its implications. It was described as a charter to "free world trade". It was found to be a charter for trade control. It required our Government to plan and control the economy of these United States; and it required the even greater control of that economy by the global authority which it was designed to create. It condemned cartels if they were private; it blessed them if they were governmental. It did *not* "free" trade; the charter did the opposite, and in scholarly accordance with socialist doctrine.

The result of its adoption would have been economic socialism, on a global plane.

Those who have examined with studious concern the organizations on the political scene will see how parallel are these organizations on the economic. The movement of the pincers will be distinct and clear.

The supranational authorities all have their counterpart in finance. The counterpart is the International Bank and Fund. All these organizations would be essential if world government were the goal. All are there.

Is this the "new era", the age of controlled economy? If it is, surely a great and precious contribution, uniquely American, is being lost. It could be a contribution to all humanity, it seems to me. And as I have said, I believe it is to be found in the substantive document of our Republic. That document, the Constitution, established our people as sovereign, and limited uncompromisingly the powers of the state—to make of it their agent. It freed the minds of men. And it was from his own free mind that man invented, and built. He pioneered, and he created. And it is from *man,* not from "government", that commerce, industry, and art emerge; it is from *man* that all human activity is freed for creativity, and is developed. And if such creation be not the attribute of a single government, it can not be that of a group of governments, or of a superstate.

It follows, therefore, that if the facts convince us, the ancient theory must be abandoned. If it does not work to *mutual* advantage, it cannot work at all. And if that be so, we must abandon this outworn theory, and re-adopt the new.

GATT

The procedure set forth in the charter of the ITO first appeared as a series of general executive proposals. These were published by the Department of State in November 1945, as *Bulletin No. 2411.* Ninety days later, on February 18, 1946, a specialized agency of the United Nations (UNESCO) agreed to sponsor an International Conference on Trade and Employment. This conference was to put the general proposals into specific form. Its delegates met in London during October of that same year.

Implicit in the State Department's original proposals were the following points:

1. The gradual elimination of tariffs;
2. A setting aside of our antitrust laws, and their subordination to an agency of the United Nations;
3. Intergovernmental commodity agreements; and
4. The planning of world production and employment, by an agency of the UN.

The delegates at the London conference extended this program. From their deliberations emerged the "Point 4" program, the Marshall Plan, and an understanding that America would embark upon a long and extended policy of "foreign aid". To the initial proposals was also added the proposition of establishing an "international Agreement Relating to Industrial Production".

The next meeting was set for Havana. It was here that the ITO charter was born.

In 1951 the President appointed a Materials Policy Commission. William S. Paley was named chairman, and the report which it made became known as the Paley Report. The Commission submitted this report in June of 1952. It was an interesting report in many ways. One was its reference to the ITO.

Presumably the ITO had been still-born; presumably it was dead. Nevertheless, alive or dead, responsibility for its provisions appeared somehow to have devolved upon the people of the United States. This responsibility did not come to them of their own free will. The responsibility was accepted for them by resolution. The resolution itself was passed by a social, political and economic authority, global in its scope. The fact of this responsibility was remote from the people's knowledge, and excluded from their control.

The Paley Report said:[1]

The United States has not ratified the [ITO] treaty, but under a resolution of the United Nations Economic and Social Council is bound with other nations to recognize chapter VI [of the ITO charter] as a general guide.

And what was Chapter VI of the supposedly dead ITO, which we were "bound with other nations to recognize"? Chapter VI originated from the *Proposals for Expansion of World Trade and Employment,*[2] which the American executive branch had published in 1945.[3] It was the section of the ITO charter which was "to assure the equitable distribution of a primary commodity in short supply."[4]

Here is illustrated the extent to which our people have allowed to lapse the principles of self-government; how America's industrialists and businessmen have lost control of normal access to primary commodities by means of which they function; how our farmers lose control when an agricultural product is declared "a primary commodity in short supply"; and how these United States have themselves lost control over normal access to prime essentials by which our people live and by which the Republic can be kept secure.

Has this normal access been lost by treaty? Not in this instance. Has it been lost by executive agreement? Again, not in this instance. It has been lost, but how? By "resolution". Whose resolution? The resolution of a single specialized agency of an international organization.

UNESCO was the specialized agency; UN was the international body.

---

[1]Materials Policy Commission, Report. *Vol. 1, p. 87.* 1952
[2]Department of State. *Bulletin No. 2411.* November, 1945
[3]International Materials Conference. Hearings, *Part IV.* 1953-4
[4]ITO charter. *Ch. VI, Art. 57, Subsec. F*

And what does this particular "resolution" declare? It declares that we, these United States of America, are "bound" by a single chapter of the international charter of a global authority which does not exist.

By the simple expedient of declaring a commodity in "short supply", a global authority can thus make or break whole sectors of our economy, and close down production vital to our Nation's defense.

And thus, beneath its velvet wrapping, is bared another of the pincers' teeth. The political slogans of "international cooperation" and of "collective security", and the economic slogans of "reciprocity" and "world trade" are seen to come together, merging into one. And this is the ultimate slogan of them all, the one around whose implications there must be no controversy, about which there must be no question, whatever may be its means and cost. As the pincers close, as the pressures rise, those caught within the movement will have lost their status as free citizens of this Republic—but they may have purchased "peace". The actual means and purchase price must not, forsooth, be questioned.

It is a "doctrine", ultimate and sublime.

The generations which follow are expected to welcome this estate, for its theory is being devotedly taught our children, in our schools. The theme is "world understanding".

The Preparatory Committee of the Conference on Trade and Employment had met in London during September of 1946. This Preparatory Committee recommended procedures to give effect "to certain provisions of the charter of the International Trade Organization by means of a General Agreement on Tariffs and Trade."

Then—and with the ink scarcely dry on the proposed 30,000-word charter of the ITO—the Preparatory Committee reconvened in Geneva. Their sessions were held from April to October, 1947. Out of this conference came the General Agreement on Tariffs and Trade. This last became known by its initials, GATT.

Originally, GATT had been planned as a complement to the ITO. The ITO charter referred but lightly to it, in a single paragraph; a mere footnote had explained that GATT was the "proposed arrangement" for the "concerted reduction" of tariffs and barriers to trade.

However, the ITO charter was discovered to contain so many provisions which were clearly inimical to the people and economy of the United States that its acceptance by the Senate seemed dubious. The charter was therefore permitted to die in committee. In this manner the ITO failed at birth. Not so with its complement, GATT.

With GATT, a different procedure was employed. The procedure was executive proclamation.

The foundations of the ITO had been carefully planned, and ground for its structure reserved. When the structure failed of creation, the space reserved remained a vacuum. Into this vacuum came GATT. The *theory* of controlled and regulated trade—foreign and domestic—was the single, dominating idea within.

In GATT, the 1934 Trade Agreements Act found ultimate expression. If GATT is permitted to remain in being, if the theory upon which it is based is not repudiated, its effect upon our people, our economy, our employment; upon our laws, our commerce and our politics, will painfully and progressively increase. I use the word "ultimate" in the sense of *basic*. It is basic—ultimate—in these two ways:

1. GATT ends our American policy of *bi*-lateral trade agreements, and adopts—finally and conclusively—the concept of multi-lateral agreements which is completely alien to our commercial life. It is an old-world concept, under which we no longer make agreements with single nations, on a basis of give-and-take. By applying the "most favored nation" clause, we extend automatically to *all* nations the concessions which are found advantageous between ourselves and one;

2. GATT, as an international entity—from which others can spring, and will—is in no way whatsoever responsible to the elected representatives of the people of these United States.

There are those who argue, and sincerely, that a "new progressive era" is upon us, and that such mechanisms as ITO and GATT are essential to that "new age"; it is further argued that from them our own people and Nation benefit equally with others, that what we may sacrifice at one point will be recompensed to us at others. On the latter I do have strong doubts, and am by no means unprepared to state them. But "benefits"—imagined or real—are not what I have in mind. What gives rise to my concern is something very different. I am deeply concerned at, and opposed to, the manner in which the entire movement itself is proceeding. And I reject outright the theory upon which it is based.

I reject, most emphatically, the idea that the elected representatives of our people are no longer to be directly responsible to the people for their acts; the idea that our representative government must lose its character, and is to be increasingly beholden to executive authority—whether national or international; that either our own executive, or that international executive authorities, can do for our people what they cannot, with representative government, do for themselves; and the idea that our citizens, individually or as associations or as corporations, are to lose the effective right to present their wishes to their elected public servants—for the astounding reason that those who are elected are to be no longer responsible to those who put them into office.

For that is the situation in cold fact, and we might just as well face it. What is at stake is the *representative* nature of our Union of sovereign States.

Back in the 1930s it seemed that our entire national structure might collapse. It seemed that, despite the magnificent success of our entirely new theory of self-government and individual self-reliance, the result must be a failure. Perhaps if we had taken more time; had we perhaps not been in such a (characteristically American) hurry, we might have seen that its flaws could with patience be removed—without impairment of our own peculiar concept and belief. We even might have found ways to not again experience such tragic collapse, and yet still adhere to our own new, American way. We might have studied that concept of ours more carefully, and found that what was happening was not the result of theory but had come about from errors in its human operation. We might have found those errors, and have proceeded to their correction while retaining the essential base upon which our body social, politic and economic for so long had rested.

We did not do that. We abandoned our new philosophy and, all unconsciously, we slid backward into the old. That philosophy had for so long been unknown to us that to many the old did seem the "new"— and we were told by some that it was. Yet it was an ancient concept, and it said: The State can do for me, and must, what I cannot do, or may be unwilling to do, for myself.

It was a theory, and for centuries it ruled all human life.

Politically, economically—and now "socially"—The State took over, as it always has done, and, when it is permitted to do so, as it always will. And as gradually The State took over, the ancient theory itself was broadened. Now it said: The International State will do together what none of its single states can do alone.

GATT was an instrument of the growing International State.

It was a "key element in the Nation's foreign economic policy", to be "carried on under the authority vested in the President by the Congress in the trade agreements legislation." GATT would make rules and regulations on tariffs and trade—and it would make concessions and exceptions. It was designed for "the orderly expansion of international trade"; its interests would include "a balanced and expanding world economy . . . [the] international flow of capital, higher standards of living, full employment". It would undertake to promote "economic and social progress".

Implicit in its vision was Cordell Hull's romantic dream. Trade would be international, and it would be "free".

Congress, it was claimed by the executive, had passed the enabling legislation when it passed the 1934 Act. No objection to GATT was heard from other nations. What GATT could not do at its inception was cause for little hesitation on their part. It could amend itself. It could, in other words, add to itself such powers as might initially not be present; it could vote unto itself such powers as it might wish. No; there was no reluctance shown by other nations. They would be in control.

At long last, the profits-laden marts of the United States had been made accessible to products made by labor which had no such high-paid standards as do ours, and opened to employers who paid them no such rates. America's industry and agriculture, always in competition with the politico-cartel arrangements of an older world, found themselves now enmeshed in the machinery of that cartel, made worldwide. A few found it possible to "play ball". And they did.

Not a word in GATT, nor in any of its proposed extensions, reveals the slightest interest in the American workingman, in the American investor, in the American farmer, or in the American citizen. And if it happened that any of these came to be adversely affected, for them a plan would later be produced.

GATT became an established fact. A steady flow of funds from the United States could now swell the gigantic pool of loans and gifts, as from an invisible spring.

This was the meaning of "Trade, not Aid".

GATT itself was our economic Yalta. At Yalta—whoever may have been responsible—the executive sold out the best of our allies. By the General Agreement on Tariffs and Trade—whoever may have been responsible—the executive sold out our own. Sooner or later, no one escapes: Not the men and women employed in the industries which are wholly or in part displaced; not the office forces; not the executives; not the owners or the investors; not the farmers or the growers; not the seamen or those who own and operate our ships; not our businessmen, not our retailers; and certainly neither you nor I, the taxpayers who foot the bills.

The claim is made that the overall program is, nevertheless, of great benefit to everyone, including us. The claim is suavely made, and it is less than easy to refute. With 64,000,000 people on gainful payrolls, who can contest the claim of "full employment"? With a gross national product of more than $400,000,000,000, who will worry about occasional gaps? Yet those who have been hit, have been hit hard. Their numbers are increasing, and they will continue to increase.

American products are being displaced in our own markets by similar products of foreign manufacture. Many of these imports are made by labor which is low-paid in comparison with wages here, and this labor abroad is operating our latest model machines. The products are coming in in foreign hulls while our own ships go out of service.

We are told that the increased volume of foreign trade results in higher living standards on the part of workingmen overseas, yet such assertions are not borne out in fact. The imported products are not competitive with our own in *social* price; the difference in invoice price is largely the difference in wages paid. In other words, our avowed policy— one which has found many sincere adherents—is to help raise living standards everywhere. The policy is increasing foreign employment, yes; it is *not* materially raising foreign wages. And what it is doing for others' employment it is accomplishing at the expense of our own.

The overall program is so designed as already to have made it advantageous for some of our factories to relocate abroad, in direct contradiction to the purposes which are publicly proclaimed. Over twenty years ago, remember, we were told that this very thing was being caused by the "impossibly high duties" of the Smoot-Hawley tariff; the relocation abroad of American factories was one of the economic ailments for which the Trade Agreements Act of 1934 was asserted to be the cure.

Our tariffs are the lowest of any major trading nation in the world. Contrary to widespread statements and belief, they have been the lowest in the world for quite some years. Yet in addition to cuts made pursuant to the Trade Agreements Act, we have made over 55,000 concessions under GATT.

Sixty percent of our imports never did pay duties; they were not in competition with our products. The duties on other imports were imposed to reserve our home markets for our own producers. One of the reasons for this protection was the relatively low pay of workers in other lands. To this has been added a new, important factor: Low-paid foreign workers now are operating the most modern machines. Do the families of America's workingmen feel they can long compete with other workingmen overseas, when the latter now have identical machines? Does any wheat or cotton grower in these United States for a moment dream that we can continue to send seed and fertilizer, money, equipment and technicians abroad—without creating self-sufficiencies in those markets, and "crop surpluses" and "soil banks" here at home?

Under GATT and other international authorities, the decision upon such matters is not reached by the people who are directly concerned. These matters are to be decided by international bodies, responsible only to themselves. Their nation-members operate, and will continue to operate, exactly as we would expect to operate if the position were reversed. Each will look out for Number One.

Acting together and in concert, they will open our markets as wide as they can, and for as long as they find it possible. For exports, their shippers will take our payments—cash. For themselves, the political authorities will continue to accept in gifts and loans that commodity which is by far our own Nation's greatest export—also cash.

Those Americans who are hurt in the process will be offered "relief". And that, as well, is cash.

The mysterious source of all this cash may not be observable to the man or woman on Main Street—until the tax-return is filed; or unless he remarks the difference between what he has earned and the amount he finds he has—after the tax-deductions from his payroll.

The Way Out

The years through which the theory of peaceful world organization has been applied—with its goal of universal acceptance of one code, one law—have been characterized by worldwide turbulence, intervention and war. How is it that a great and intelligent Nation has not, so far, effectively reappraised the causative theory itself, and offered for mature consideration a concept which might work?

In view of the colossal sacrifice involved—in men and in real wealth —the theory required influential acceptance and support from the start. Two courses were adopted to realize it, and they were these: (1) Individuals and organizations, public and private, were found and to them was presented the glittering promise of a new utopia; and (2) an historical blackout which amounted almost to continuing censorship was gradually contrived. The first of these courses was open and aboveboard; the other was quietly done, and it took time. Eventually it made "controversial"—even incredible—such books as this, however documented might be their facts.

These two courses, together with their scores of ramifications, kept people from visualizing the gigantic pincers movement which the theory itself required. First the depression, then wars and the preparation for wars, diverted people from the gradual impact of the movement itself. Propaganda did the rest.

The New York *Journal of Commerce* of October 17, 1955 stated that our national income during the second quarter of that year was running at a rate of $321 billion per annum, a new high. *Business in Brief,* the Chase Manhattan Bank's quarterly, stated in its issue of October 1955 that our gross national product for the third quarter was running at a rate of $391 billion per annum. At the same time, the Federal budget was at $73 billion for the year.

This means that 18.5 percent of the national product—22.74 percent of the national income—is being siphoned off by Federal taxes alone. Not a penny for local, county or State taxes is included. In Indiana, the people paid more taxes in 1956 for "foreign aid" alone than they paid to run the entire State government and administration.

Meanwhile, we face the dictum that laws which are made in accordance with a State constitution, or in accordance with the United States Constitution, are not to be applied if they conflict with the "principles and purposes of the United Nations". We discover that a simple "resolution", adopted by UNESCO, can "bind" our people and Nation, even though—as we have learned—this "resolution" is based upon a single chapter of the international charter of a global authority which did not exist (the ITO).

The theory says that at any given time there is one bad nation which threatens civilization (1914, Germany; 1939, Germany; 1945, the U.S.S.R.). And there is one outstanding corollary to this notion, one which we learn is this: We are appointed the knight in shining armor; we shall see to it that that bad nation sins no more.

The theory requires our constant intervention, and the result is that every local war carries within it the fatal germ of international conflict. Following this theory in hopeful urgency, we have made treaties, agreements and military alliances, and we have made commitments to a global organization which by its very being involves us directly or indirectly in each and every such local war. We underwrite dying empires at that very moment in history when the imperial system is as dead as Julius Caesar, and when those empires' component parts are themselves emerging painfully into independence. The fact that those components sooner or later are going to achieve their independence, the fact that we are being called upon to back inevitable "losers", is a point only in passing history. The big point is that we are by our acts denying to others the very aspirations which brought about the creation of our own Republic. We, who were the first to sever the ties of empire, are now become its defenders—though if we continue to follow this theory we will be the pallbearers at its tragic demise.

We have sent the men and women of our Armed Forces into over sixty countries. We build apartment houses and schools for their families overseas, and by the Status of Forces agreement we deprive them of their basic rights of citizenship and subject them to foreign courts and law.

We have created a military establishment designed not only to protect the rightful interests of our own, we have been persuaded to accept a theory which requires that our youth be charged with the mission to protect the world. This global Department of Defense in 1955 employed 4,300,000 people—nearly 7 percent of our active labor force. The original cost of that Department's assets was some 140 billion dollars. It owned almost 31 million acres of land; it operated some 2,500 separate business enterprises and the assets of these latter totalled over 15 billion dollars. The general officers of Army, Navy and Air are charged with global responsibilities for which no man should be expected to answer—tactically, strategically or logistically.

We have loaned and given, and spent in foreign countries, a total which may never be known but which already is estimated at something like a hundred billion dollars*—all out of the pockets of our working citizens. We have agreed that our tariffs be cut and cut and cut. We are importing the goods of commerce at a rate half again as great as in 1948-9, while the percentage of our own exportable goods which are being shipped abroad as *commercial* trade is less than it was in 1934.

---

*Publisher's Note: The usually reliable *Washington News Bulletin* (Paul O. Peters, Editor) listed such outlays by year in its No. 232 of Nov. 19, 1957. The totals were:

Grants and credits, war period	$ 59,869,639,312
Grants and credits, post-war	73,469,451,624
Total Grants	$133,339,090,936
Estimated costs of money borrowed to finance foreign aid	20,000,000,000
Estimated gross cost of foreign aid to June 30, 1957	$153,339,090,936

Allowable deductions (reverse lend-lease, repayments, and surplus property payments)

War-period total ..	$ 2,427,348,507
Post-war period ..	7,834,277,239
Total	$10,261,625,746 —10,261,625,746

Net cost of foreign aid, to June 30, 1957 .... $143,077,465,190

(Compiled from figures issued by the Office of Business Economics and predecessor agencies, U. S. Dept. of Commerce)

By our policies we have narrowed the annual "dollar-gap"* to $4.8 billion, the figures given for 1955. And the $4.8 billion "gap" was taken care of (by us) in this way: $2.8 billion for military outlays abroad, for overseas bases and for "offshore procurement"; $1.5 to $2.0 billion of net new overseas investment, including remittances; and about $2.0 billion in "economic aid". "Thus", says the issue of *Business in Brief* cited above, "the 'dollar gap' is not a significant problem for the time being."

The same issue goes on to say that " . . . the Administration program for further orderly reductions in tariffs (which have been cut more than 50% since 1934)† and for customs simplification should help support a rise in our foreign trade." The "Administration" did not see fit to confide in us the fact just cited, that our commercial export trade was less, percentagewise, than it had been back in 1934 when the program started.

Nor will the extension of the "Administration program" be worked out by elected representatives of our people; it will be worked out and put into effect by an international authority-cartel. The international authority-cartel is responsible only to itself.

The way out of the situation is an essential and a simple one. The situation has come about through the working of a theory, and the economic phases of this theory began with the Trade Agreements Act of 1934. Pages of endless figures, long arguments *pro* and *con,* can but serve to confound the issue. The issue is the theory itself.

The theory is that The State can do for a citizen what *it* determines he cannot do for himself; that The International State can do for our Nation what *it* determines we as a Nation are incapable of accomplishing ourselves.

The rest follows. As a state's decisions are feckless without the means to enforce them, clearly The State must find ways to power. This much clear within the theory, there remained the matter of procedure; and this, as well, was clear.

Power must first be vested in The State, and then it must be transferred to The International State. This presented no problem abroad— The State already had the power. In our Country the sovereign power rested in the people, so this power had first to be taken from them, *i.e.,* from the representatives whom they elected.

This first step was accomplished when the Congress abdicated,

---

*When a nation lives beyond its income in dollar trade, or when it fixes a "value" on its currency which is higher in relation to dollars than what the currency actually is worth, the resulting annual deficit is called a "dollar-gap".

†The actual reduction by 1955 was approximately 68%.

in 1934. The American executive then progressively transferred that power to international bodies, and the thing was done.

The theory could now be applied on a global scale. It eventually would be as all-encompassing as was the total power which formed its base.

There are those, I know, who hold that much good has been accomplished by its application. My viewpoint differs, and in what I feel is a basic sense. I believe that there is a right theory, and a wrong theory, for us to follow. And I believe that in every instance where those who feel that the program is a good program and has been of benefit to the world, the result could have been achieved otherwise than it has, and in a different way. It could have followed procedures inherent in the new American concept, where the people themselves determine their course of action. A strict adherence to that concept would have averted the adoption, by us, of the ancient, reactionary theory that people must leave the governing power to those who are not responsible directly to them.

And therein lies the essential, simple way out—abandon the time-worn theory of Power-in-the-State.

The people of these United States must dynamically restore their effective representative government, and make its actions—the actions of their own representatives—once more beholden to them.

Then no longer will they be told—by others—what is good for them, and what is not.

They will determine the matter for themselves.

PART II

RESULTS OF THE ECONOMIC PINCERS MOVEMENT

How has the theory applied since 1934 affected our economy? How have its results followed upon its proclaimed intent? I suggest that you now turn back to page 14 and read again the claims advanced in favor of the initial legislation and have them clearly in your mind, in relation to the facts which will be laid before you.

Keep in mind, too, that a tariff is properly employed for just three reasons: For revenue, to protect the legitimate economy, and to ensure the nation's self-defense. It is not a "weapon". At least, Americans have not thought of it as a weapon.

When we sit down at the conference table with others, what is *their* concept of the tariff? How do *they* employ it? Do they have other procedures at their disposal, and may any of these procedures actually be conceived as weapons? If so, what are some of them? How are they employed?

We sit down at an economic conference. We have a tariff, which can be adjusted. In return for such adjustment we would like certain markets reasonably opened to our wares. Around the table sit others. They, quite naturally, are interested in our markets, and in our cash. We want something; others want something. The conference is to see if and where these wants can meet. The object is "world trade". To the extent that the wants are normally and reasonably compatible, the result can be *legitimate* world trade.

The conferees confer. They follow their agenda. Agreements are reached. Tariffs will be lowered. The news is given to the world of trade, and announcements are read by millions of others who are not directly engaged in trade. Trade benefits everyone in some way so these others will benefit, too.

The United States proceeds to lower its rates on the commodities upon which agreement has been reached by the conferees. This is not done by the Congress, to be sure; contrary to the mandate of the Constitution, it is done by the executive. But it is done. Imports of these commodities increase. What happens elsewhere? Does the increase work both ways?

Let us imagine that tariffs elsewhere are cut on the agreed commodities, for at times the cuts are made, pursuant to the agreement. Tariffs have been cut, then. So far, so good.

But that is only "so far".

The bargaining power of America—the tariff—has been nullified, to use a word, when our delegates agree to cuts. They have used up their bargaining power. The markets of America have to that extent been exchanged. Exchanged for what? Exchanged for compensating tariff concessions, to increase "world trade". Now, however, come into play certain factors. These factors may not be held as "weapons" by our friends, but their effect upon us, upon our trade, is not unlike the effect would be if that were our friends' idea. Among these factors are the following:

As many as thirty different kinds of currency may be authorized by a single nation at a single, given time. There is "import" money, "export" money, "tourist" money; there are "import licenses" and there is "licensed exchange"; there are "blocked balances" and "counterpart funds"; there is an "official" rate of exchange and there is the "unofficial" rate of exchange. All these, and more, can be used to counteract the "reciprocal" advantage of a cut in tariff granted to ourselves. All of them are used.

A government will require that x percentage of its imports be carried in its own ships. Earnings from this carrying trade compensate for tariff concessions. However, by simple decree, one of our friends may now announce that as of a given date the percentage of imports carried by its ships must be 2 times x. Upon the shoulders of our shipping men (including our seamen "on the beach") immediately falls the economic burden of the new concessions.

The governments of our friends step in further. They place quotas on, they even ban completely, commodities upon which a tariff has been lowered in exchange for our concessions. In this event, we get the lowered rates, and we do little trade or none at all.

There is another idea which our friends employ, and it has to do with "specifications". The tariff on y commodity has been lowered, a concession has been made to the Americans. But other commodities are produced or made elsewhere and these foreign products have characteristics not usual with competing lines produced in the U.S.A. So our friends draw up specifications. For example: A nation specifies that only trucks and automobiles of a certain weight may run on the roads of its colonial possessions. Oddly, this particular nation is the only one which makes such automobiles or trucks. This very wrinkle has been used in Bermuda, where only automobiles of British design fit the specifications.

These are a few of the factors which are employed, and about which "the Administration" in pursuing its program, does not speak. American delegates to trade conferences know these things, and mention them at such conferences. All the delegates then agree that such practices are bad. So tariff cuts are accompanied by a unanimous statement of principles. There is an agreement drawn up, and in it are written promises specific and promises vague. These promises and principles are then shown to Congressmen and other people as evidence of progress toward "freeing world trade". Our tariff cuts remain.

Much is said about the export trade in American machinery. Few have objection to such trade. Much of this export has been paid for by our own tax-money, to be sure, but that is not my point. Machinery is run and operated by *men*. Men are labor. And when the product of one of these American machines is, in turn, imported back into our own market it means that we have exported labor. Where the products of this machinery can be made efficiently and properly here (at a competitive American price), every single product which is imported displaces just so much work otherwise available to a man right here. The same is true of agriculture's "surplus crops", and its result is acreage restriction —by The State.

Incidentally, the corollary of free trade is free immigration and world-wide integration. Advocates of the policy are silent on this reality.

The export of employment goes yet further. Entire factories are being exported. Again, the fact that we furnish to our friends the money with which they erect plants, to in turn manufacture equipment which our friends ship to countries situated within the Soviet empire, is incidental. The matter is broader than that.

In 1947 I talked with Sir Stafford Cripps in England. That was in November, and we were discussing the Marshall Plan. I said to him: "I understand from my figures that you are 114 percent recovered on the industrial index at this time." He hesitated just a moment, and then replied: "That is true . . . . We do not need the money in England so badly, but we need it to build new industries in Africa, in our possessions in Africa." So I asked Sir Stafford this: "Mr. Cripps, do you mean for our Government to give your Government money to build industries and transportation and so forth, in Africa, in your possessions there, and that they would be clear of debt and your Government would own them?" And he said, "Yes."

So there I was. Our own people ("our Government") were giving funds to a socialist government; the funds would be frankly used to construct state-owned factories and transportation in a distant part of its colonial empire. And this program was supposed to "combat communism"!

Twenty years it had taken this pattern to unfold. And such is its design that now we find entire industries transferring their American plants abroad, or constructing new plants overseas. And if you are asked "Why not?" I would say there is no reason in the world—if it is done in pursuit of private initiative, responsibility, risk and enterprise. But when an American industry transfers its plant and its employment abroad, and then ships its products back into the American market as a direct result of the policy of our own Government, that policy is shown not to be based upon what is good, right and proper for the citizens whose government it is.

Furthermore, citizens who are investing funds in enterprises abroad are being offered the guarantee of the return of their investments, and of their profits, as encouragements to do so. A result of this is naturally to broaden the support of the policy by increasing the numbers of those who appear to benefit directly by it. Yet here is the procedure of "state capitalism", a procedure not even remotely to be associated with private American enterprise. Is it not clear that The State which "grants" such inducements can also, at its pleasure, take those inducements away?

There is the ever-present appeal of humanitarianism, I know. But I believe this applies to Americans, too. Our cash and finance can be put in envelopes, and mailed; not so with our employment, with our working-men.

The foregoing do not constitute assertions in support of some vague program. They are facts. These facts come from the application of a theory, and the theory was implicit in the 1934 Trade Agreements Act. Those who feel that they still can successfully deny the impact of that theory are invited to compare its actual results with the attractive promises with which it was ushered in.*

A Few Specific Cases

I have suggested that you turn back these pages and compare the claims with which this program was ushered in, with the results which have since accrued. For years now, some of us have been actively opposing the entire procedure. Among others, I myself am on record as having predicted these results. Which was right? The claims of those who brought about this policy, of those who urged that Congress abdicate and permit the executive to take over in 1934? Or are the opposing claims proving right—the claims of those who stood against such flagrant violation of the Constitution's mandate, and who warned of what would ensue if representative government were to revert to rulership by The State?

The Congressional abdication in the 1934 Trade Agreements Act was specific. It violated the basic principle of representative government; it was reactionary in the fullest sense. It abdicated to the executive (The State) a power over the economic life of the citizenry; it deprived the citizen of his Constitutional right to control the acts of his own officials.

The executive was to act at its own unfettered discretion.

This unfettered discretion has been applied "for the benefit" of the Nation's economy. A number of cases will show how that "benefit" is being felt.

Textiles. In May 1955 the Department of Labor reported that there were 156 distressed areas scattered throughout these United States. This was 12 more distressed areas than there had been sixty days before; it was 76 more distressed areas than there had been a year before; it was 119 more distressed areas than there had been two years before.

Textile manufacture was the No. 1 industry in 20 of these distressed areas, and it was the second dominant industry in 5 more.

When the Trade Agreements Act was submitted to Congress in 1955 for another three-year extension, few of the unemployed textile workers

_____
*Cf. page 14.

of New England, of the Middle Atlantic States or of the South were able to appear as witnesses against the extension.

Coal. Of the 156 distressed areas listed by the Department of Labor in 1955, coal mining was the No. 1 industry in thirty-three.

Coal mining is suffering from the impact of tremendous imports of foreign waste oils, including shipments from the Middle East and Indonesia. These shipments are being dumped on our eastern shores. The situation would be worse were it not for the export of American coal to countries which, like Britain, formerly were large producers for their own export trade. America has actually been shipping coal to Newcastle, and in large quantities.

Unemployed coal miners in Pennsylvania and West Virginia could not go to Washington and appear at hearings, to protest against the three-year extension of the Act.

Shipbuilding — the American Carrying Trade

During the second world war we built the *Liberty*-type ship, and reciprocating engines were installed in them. Every marine engineer who sailed them knows that they were obsolete before they were built. At the same time, we supplied turbines and diesels to other nations, and these engines of the very latest types were installed in foreign-built ships. When the war was over, these vessels were ready for the fast competitive carrying trade. Our *Liberty* ships, with their reciprocating engines, went into the mothball fleet.

Then, following the war, we turned to the *Mariner*-type vessel. This ship was soon being returned by private operators to the Maritime Commission as "too expensive to operate". One company, after having flown the American Flag for 92 years, has replaced its entire fleet of *C-1s* and *C-2s* with smaller, more economical vessels—all of them built in foreign yards. These ships now fly a foreign flag.

According to *Maritime Affairs* for August 1953, only two percent of the total new tonnage built between 1947 and July 1952, was built for United States Flag registry. Leigh R. Sanford, president of the Shipbuilders Council of America, says, "There have been no orders for seagoing merchant ships for our foreign trade placed in any coastal ship-yard in the United States during 1953, from any source." No passenger ship, and no passenger-cargo ship, was built in American yards in 1953 or 1954.

Let us now look at *The Log,* Annual Maritime Reference Yearbook Number, August 31, 1955 (Vol. 50, No. 9). Here is the picture which it draws of maritime activity during the preceding twelve months:

1. The merchant fleets of all principal maritime nations *except* the United States increased in size and carrying capacity;

2. A noticeable increase of waterborne commerce took place during the eight months immediately preceding the report;

3. There was a *decrease* in the number of vessels flying the United States Flag, but *no* decrease in the number of vessels owned by American citizens;

4. 118 vessels, of 904,111 gross tons, were transferred and/or sold to foreign flags, but many of them continued to be owned or controlled by American citizens under a foreign corporation;

5. The tonnage owned or controlled by American or affiliated interests increased during the twelve months by vessels built for American interests in foreign yards and for registry under a foreign flag— American interests now own more merchant shipping than any other national group;

6. A considerable percentage of the 950 merchant vessels totalling 7,825,000 gross tons currently flying Panamá, Liberia or Honduras flags are owned or controlled in the United States. Low taxes, wages and operating costs make possible these "flags of convenience".

Since the second world war, the sale or transfer of privately owned American Flag merchant vessels reached its high point in 1950, a year which was exceeded only in 1939-40-41. In addition, under the terms of the Merchant Ship Sales Act of 1946, there were 1,113 merchant vessels sold abroad by the Maritime Commission, and their total gross tonnage was 7,923,308. Of 118 ship-transfers during 1954, 91 went to Liberia, 16 to Panamá, 5 to Honduras, 3 to Great Britain, 2 to Japan and 1 to China. 1,862 American built vessels have been transferred to foreign flags since 1938, to a total of 12,287,631 gross tons. Shipbuilding costs in the United States which were at 100% in 1939 had risen to 230% by 1955.

No passenger ships had been built in American yards either in 1953 or 1954. The slow-moving (reciprocating engine) *Liberty*-type ship was costing $900 a day to operate; the same ship cost $254 a day under the Liberian flag. "The principal cause for the great increase in the number of vessels transferred to foreign flag was the general contraction in the volume of freight available to American flag ship owners, principally those in the tramp trades moving bulk cargoes."⁕

⁕See the memorial to Congress from the crew of the *S. S. Louisiana*. (*Bibliography*, p. 116)

Since the end of the war, 626 ships, aggregating 3,837,629 gross tons, were scrapped in America. The average age of United States Flag ships was about 10 years. (Pp. 116, 130, 141)

Two sets of figures show graphically the state of the vitally essential fleets of oceangoing ships which fly the American Flag, and compare the figures with those of other nations:

NEW CONSTRUCTION IN HAND OR ON ORDER IN PRINCIPAL COUNTRIES,
1,000 GROSS TONS OR OVER, AS OF APRIL 1, 1955

	Cargo and Colliers, Ore Carriers, etc.		Tankers		Passenger, and Combined Passenger and Cargo		TOTALS	
	Vessels	Gr. Tons	Vessels	Gr. Tons	Vessels	Gr. Tons	Vessels	Gr. Tons
All countries	953	5,442,068	390	5,997,990	59	539,630	1,402	11,979,688
U.S.A.	4	32,900	11	171,860	..	..	15	204,760

COUNTRY OF CONSTRUCTION AND FLAG OF REGISTRY OF NEW MERCHANT VESSELS OVER 1,000 GROSS TONS, EXCLUSIVE OF VESSELS BUILT FOR OPERATION ON THE GREAT LAKES OR INLAND WATERWAYS, FOR THE ARMED FORCES, OR SPECIAL TYPES SUCH AS TUGS, FERRIES, CABLE SHIPS, ETC.

	Cargo and Colliers, Ore Carriers, etc.		Tankers		Passenger, and Combined Passenger and Cargo		TOTALS	
	Vessels	Gr. Tons	Vessels	Gr. Tons	Vessels	Gr. Tons	Vessels	Gr. Tons
All countries	356	1,777,000	243	3,026,000	21	261,000	620	5,064,000
U.S.A.	10	92,000	15	225,000	..		25	317,000

The Log, as cited; pp. 110, 112

Other Industries

Electrical Machinery. Electrical machinery was the top industry in seven of the 156 distressed areas listed in May 1955 by the Department of Labor. It was the second industry in five more of those areas, and a major industry in still another. Unemployment in our machinery industries, reflecting injury caused by competitive imports from abroad, had brought distress to 19 areas and contributed to distress in nine others.

Electrical machinery was manufactured in 13 of these areas, non-electrical machinery in 10, and farm machinery in five.

Chemical Manufacture. The chemical industry was suffering unemployment in four of the areas. Wages in this industry are quadruple what they are in Britain; five times what they are in Germany. One American company (Monsanto) in 1955 negotiated a *rise* in wages, pensions and associated costs which was almost equal to its total hourly rate (about 15c) paid to workers in its plants in Japan.

Lead and Zinc: Mining. In 1955, ninety percent of the zinc and lead miners in the United States were walking the streets, unemployed.

The United States provided Britain with funds with which to purchase a stockpile of the metals. Britain bought the lead and zinc. Then, in 1953, Britain began to release the stockpile to the United States. At what price? At six cents a pound under the market. Thus Britain was given—by us—the money to buy a stockpile, and then given—by us—the funds for its re-purchase.

The market at that time was 16c a pound. At that figure, owners here could make a profit; small to be sure, but still a profit. Our miners would be working, earning their $15 to $18 a day. But we bought these metals—mostly from foreign mines—at 10c a pound, and the perfectly natural result occurred. Our mines shut down.

In the past two years American production has been cut in half—only the high-production mines can operate.

The Tariff Commission—still nominally an agency of Congress—heard the case, and it recommended tariff-relief. Tariff-relief was not granted. The executive branch turned down the findings, and turned down the recommendations. They did not accord with "our foreign policy".

Mercury. This small but important industry held its own in competition with imported mercury for more than eighty years, prior to 1939. The outbreak of war skyrocketed demand and at the same time cut off supplies from Italy and Spain. As in other fields, America came to the rescue and not only was self-sufficient in mercury but furnished 20,000 flasks* of it to the Soviet. Then came "peace".

A cartel, formed in Europe, openly boasted it was going to capture the world market. Its price was fixed at $300 a flask; the ceiling price in the United States was $191. To this American price situation the cartel addressed itself. Its resultant procedure was drastic and direct.

The cartel dropped its price to $45 a flask, f.a.s. New York. The American tariff was absorbed by the (foreign) producer. By 1950 all Mexican and Canadian production had ceased, and our own domestic production fell to its lowest ebb in a hundred years.

Now began the fun. The cartel raised its price to $200 a flask. During the Korean crisis its price was $240. On June 1, 1954, the price was hiked again, to $265.

An industry had been forced to abandon its activity in Mexico, Canada and the United States. Men were forced to seek new employment. Users and consumers received no savings in price. Taxes were lost

---

*A "flask" of mercury weighs 76 pounds.

locally, and State and nationwide. And—the pincers movement—for yet another strategic material this Nation became dependent upon foreign sources in time of war.

An analogous situation has been developing in the paper industry.

Gold, Fluorspar, Tungsten, Manganese and other American mining industries are in identical situations, differing only in degree.

The Fishing Industry. Five or six years ago a trend developed in the fishing industry, and this trend is basically attributable to the overall policy. It is of a pattern with the spot-unemployment and distress in other fields.

In 1951, there were 214 large tuna clippers operating out of San Diego, California. By the beginning of 1956 this number was down to 158. Tuna landings were $17,000,000 less in value in 1955 than they had been the year before. Tropical tuna, our most valuable deep-sea catch for years, had lost its lead position.

The sardine fishery of southern California, until ten years ago the largest fish industry in the Nation, is no longer even mentioned among the leaders. Monterey, for years our greatest fish-landing port, is no longer among the first ten. The once prosperous catch of bonito, swordfish and sharks is no more; because of foreign "competition" our own men cannot afford to go to sea for them.

The shrimp fisheries of the south Atlantic States and the Gulf of Mexico have begun an inevitable decline as the production of newly established foreign fisheries comes onto our domestic market.

The crab and salmon fisheries of the Pacific Northwest and Alaska are suffering from inadequate programs of research and conservation, while "foreign policy" dictates the channels of "world trade".

The lobster fisheries of Maine, and the great New England fishing industry, are steadily declining as cheap lobster tails and other catches come in as imports. In 1955 the Maine sardine catch was the lowest since 1940.

On the Great Lakes the story is the same. And while there are other factors which are involved, the overall program's impact is common to them all.

No one from the thousands of distressed American fishermen's homes and families could come to Washington to describe his fellows' plight, and protest against the extension of the Trade Agreements Act.

Further Industries. America's industries are not simply being affected by the importation of luxury items, or by specialized items of import for which there is an entirely legitimate case. The hurt is basic, economic and strategic.

The pressure of the economic jaw of the pincers is being increasingly felt by the following industries: Lumber, pottery, leather, watchmaking, clocks, gloves, glassware, mica, bicycles, automobiles and petroleum products. The list is not complete.*

Agriculture; Farm Products

Cotton. Exports of cotton during the 14 years prior to passage of the 1934 Trade Agreements Act averaged more than 7,000,000 bales a year. The peak year was 1926, when over 11,000,000 bales were shipped out. With the passage of that Act cotton exports dropped in the prewar years to less than 5,000,000 bales per year. From 1946 through 1953 our annual cotton exports averaged 4,234,500 bales. Exports for 1952 and 1953 were 3,110,000 bales and 3,798,000 bales respectively.

On August 1, 1955 the cotton surplus was estimated at 10.6 million bales, including 8.1 million bales which were held by the Government or

---

*PUBLISHER'S NOTE: As the pressures mount, "distressed areas" are appearing. Later in his text, Senator Malone names some of them as they are listed by the Department of Labor. Legislation has been introduced to provide for such areas as they develop. The parallel between this legislation and practices in Britain and the U.S.S.R. is illustrated by *S. 2892*, introduced in the Eighty-fourth Congress, First Session, by Sen. Smith of New Jersey. This bill was called the Area Assistance Act of 1956. It died in the Senate Banking and Currency Committee and for it was substituted *S. 2663*, the Area Redevelopment Act of 1956. *S. 2663* passed the Senate on July 26 but was not acted upon by the House.

The Smith bill provided for federal "assistance" to communities "suffering substantial unemployment" according to the Secretary of Labor; for the creation of new opportunities; for grants, loans, technical assistance, housing; for studies of the "characteristics" of the labor force in such areas; for vocational education; for "provisions for the disposition of any land in the project area", and for the "completion of such project notwithstanding any determination made after the execution of such contract that the area in which the project is located may no longer be an area of substantial and persistent unemployment." The Smith bill would empower "the storage, treatment, purification, or distribution of water, sewage, sewage treatment, and sewer facilities; and gas distribution systems for which there is an urgent and vital public need."

The Act would appoint an Area Assistance Administrator, and (an initial) revolving fund of $50,000,000. The Administrator's findings and determinations, under "such regulations as he may prescribe", shall be final, "and shall not be subject to review in any court by mandamus or otherwise."

With the convening of the Eighty-fifth Congress, Sen. Douglas of Illinois introduced the Area Redevelopment Act of 1957 on January 29. This bill is essentially a duplication of *S. 2892*. Copies may be obtained from any member of the Senate.

(Sections of *S. 2892* cited above are: 2; 101(a)1,2; 101(b)1,2; 102(a)1,2; 102(b) and 102(c); 103; 104; 105; 106; 107; 108; 110 and 111(a))

TRADE ADJUSTMENT ACT OF 1957. Introduced on Aug. 30 as *S. 2907* by Senator Kennedy of Massachusetts, this Bill has many features in common with the above, and is specifically related to the destructive impact of the Trade Agreements legislation. In Senator Kennedy's own words: The assistance which it proposes is "made necessary by the trade policy of the United States . . . " "The sudden economic reversal which these industries suffer is the result of governmental action in lowering tariffs. It is therefore the responsibility of the Government to at least lighten the blow."

were under Government loan. An additional 2.8 million bales were expected to be added to this huge pile as a result of the 1955 surplus crop.*
A million bales of short-staple cotton were offered to exporters at the beginning of 1956. By the end of February the million bales had been sold, at approximately the going world price—between 6c and 8c a pound below the American market price.

The global theory has not benefited American cotton.

Tobacco. Sixteen of our forty-eight States grow tobacco. Tobacco is the most valuable crop in six of these States. Three quarters of a million farming families take in over a billion dollars a year for their crop. Tobacco follows wheat, cotton and corn; it is America's fourth largest farm crop. Municipalities tax its products to the tune of $30,000,000 a year; States tax them for $500,000,000; the Federal Government's tax-take on tobacco exceeds $1,500,000,000 a year. This is the excise tax alone, and its total is over $2,000,000,000 a year.

Tobacco would have carried two-thirds of the operating expenses of our National Government only four decades ago at this rate! Between 1945 and 1956, cigarette taxes yielded over fifteen thousand million dollars. For more than 30 years the Federal excise tax alone has exceeded all the money received by all tobacco manufacturers for all the products they make and sell; the Federal Government has taken in taxes more than three times as much money as has been paid all the farmers who have grown the leaf from which the product taxed was itself produced.

Exports of tobacco during the 14 years preceding passage of the Trade Agreements Act averaged more than 500,000,000 pounds a year. The record was set in 1929, when over 600,000,000 pounds were shipped abroad. After the Act was passed, tobacco exports dropped to an average of 369,000,000 pounds a year before the war. Since the war, foreign shipments have averaged around 480,000,000 pounds a year, 20,000,000 pounds less than the average before the Trade Agreements Act.

Foreign government monopolies, their tariffs, their quotas, and all the controls which are employed to restrict its importation, have been unable to compensate for the people's demand for fine American tobacco abroad—even at the prices which they are obliged to pay. Trade practices abroad have simply reduced its importation by 20,000,000 pounds. At the same time, the executive government in Washington over the past ten years has reduced the acreage allotted to the American grower by 40 percent; and by dictation of the variety of tobacco which may be planted

---

*The Wall Street Journal, November 9, 1955.

has shrunk the grower's gainful crop by as much as 1,000 pounds per acre thus allotted.

The global theory has not helped the export of our tobacco.

Butter. During the 14 years prior to the passage of the Trade Agreements Act, butter exports averaged 4,777,000 pounds a year. During the seven ensuing years they averaged 2,514,000 pounds. During 1952 and 1953 the export figures were 387,000 pounds and 521,000 pounds respectively. This drop—well over 80 percent—is in export trade, which the policy was stated to "improve".

Now we are importing foreign butter.

But the outrageous corollary of the global theory is that it is obliging our taxpayers to purchase butter which they never see, and which they never eat. The "government" buys the butter; the "government" stores it. Then, every so often, we hear some prominent official propose that "we"—*i.e.,* the government—sell (or give) stored butter to a foreign nation at half the price which we ourselves have paid for it. Nothing is said of storage, spoilage or shipment costs. All of these are paid by taxes.

The global theory has not helped our "trade" in butter.

Wheat. Exports of wheat before passage of the Trade Agreements Act (without foreign aid or other forms of surplus disposal abroad) averaged 214,784,000 bushels a year. During the following seven years, wheat exports averaged 55,887,000 bushels a year. Since the war, export figures on wheat are not broken down by the executive; they do not show how much is legitimate export trade and how much has been financed in whole or in part through subsidies or "aid". The combined figure for 1953 was 219,359,000 bushels. This is approximately the average of the pre-Trade Agreements years.

The global theory has not helped our legitimate export trade in wheat.

Rye. Exports of rye before passage of the 1934 Act averaged 19,524,000 bushels a year. For the next seven years exports of rye averaged 1,231,000 bushels a year. During the first postwar years the average went to 3,164,000 bushels a year. In 1952 the export of rye was 320,000 bushels. In 1953 the export was 7,000 bushels.

Where has the overall program helped our export trade in rye?

Oats. For 10 years prior to the depression the export of oats averaged 17,039,000 bushels a year. During the depression years just prior to the passage of the Trade Agreements Act in 1934, the average export of oats was 3,778,000 bushels. The average until 1941 remained at 3,782,000 bushels a year. Exports following the war jumped to 12,979,000 bushels a year until 1948. Since 1948 the export of oats has declined each year to 3,448,000 in 1953. Clearly the global theory has not helped our export trade in oats.

Is there too much cotton? Is there too much tobacco, butter, wheat, rye, oats? I do not know; I do not claim to know. But I am aware of this: A theory cannot be right when after twenty years of operation the facts are such as these. Nor are these facts remote and far away. They concern us all, right here. My only regret is their necessarily meager presentation; they will be authenticated, and considerably amplified, by citizens and industries directly concerned.

Proponents of the theory behind our foreign policy oppose a tariff to protect the products of our own labor and, on the other hand, actively subscribe to every measure for price-support if it applies to our own domestic scene. Their logic escapes me.

What is "government-purchase"; what is "government price-support"? It seems to me that each is an exact counterpart of a tariff. And the tariff, they object, is a levy which artificially at the expense of the many protects the few.

There is, of course, this difference: A tariff can raise revenue, help support government, and assume its share of taxes; we pay a higher market-price—*once*. Subsidies, supports and "surplus" purchases come *out* of revenue. So we pay the taxes which have been used to subsidize, and we also pay the higher market price. Thus, for this *domestic* tariff-counterpart, we pay *twice*.

The domestic tariff-counterpart has its sequel, in logic and in fact. It does not fall on the foreign producer, on him who pays no taxes for our schools, our libraries, our public services, our Government, our defense, or for interest on our national debt. This tariff-counterpart is levied upon us, right here. By whom is it levied? By "government". To whom does it go? To men in business, in commerce and in trade; to men on farms and on our waterways; to men in industry, in management, in office staffs. All of these men have been jockeyed into a position where they are accepting a tariff-in-reverse.

The names by which we know it are "subsidy", "surplus purchase", and "support".

If you are displaced by the overall program, if you are out of work, the payment is called "relief"—for which, too, you are dependent upon The State.

Thus again—and in accordance with the theory—the "government" is the ruling force. Thus again the theory has required the power of The State.

In the realm of commerce, the theory requires "free trade" with nations abroad and a "protective tariff" within our Land. Our citizen-taxpayers are paying for both.

In September 1955 the Government announced it would offer for sale some of its stocks of surplus wool. A hundred and fifty million pounds of it were offered. Bought up at the taxpayers' expense, stored at taxpayers' expense, the wool was offered in monthly lots of 6¼ million pounds.

At the same time, the Government held in storage millions of pounds of dried milk, purchased at from 13c to 15c a pound. After years of storing, the Government offered one hundred and forty-seven million pounds of the product at below 9c a pound. The purchased holdings of agricultural products then in storage totalled into the *billions* of pounds.

The New York *Journal of Commerce* of September 22, 1955, said:

Losses incident to the operation of the U. S. agricultural price-support program totalled $800 million in the fiscal year ended June 30, 1955; this was almost double the $419 million loss of a year earlier. Losses arise principally from donations at home and abroad of surplus farm commodities and from sales of commodities at less than the cost of purchase. The Department of Agriculture had $7.1 billion invested in farm surpluses at the end of fiscal 1955, compared with $6 billion a year earlier.

This illustrates what is happening.

Agriculture — and the Pincers Move

If it is suggested to the executive that some alteration be made in an international agreement which is proposed, a normal alteration designed to protect America's interests, what happens? A vast publicity mill is instantly put in motion. People are informed that some "obstructionist" is getting in the way of "international cooperation". They are told that some other nation will be "hurt", that it will not "understand". We must continue to "make sacrifices for the common good". If the "obstructionists" have their way, the results will be dire indeed.

When industry representatives come to Washington and say, for instance, that the low tariff on bicycles or watches is hurting them, what happens? The publicity mill is push-buttoned into action. People are informed that Britain and Holland "look with grave misgivings" at such normal protective action on our part, that Switzerland "will not understand".

No longer does a select committee of the Congress hear the argument, and then determine its course of action. The final course of action is determined by non-elected personnel in the executive branch. What is their procedure? They listen attentively—or not—to the Americans' case. They receive the Tariff Commission's report. Then they turn it down. It does not fit into our foreign policy; it is against the overall theory being pursued.

The unemployed, the men and women who are displaced, cannot go to Washington. No one even hears of them. They write their Congressman, of course. And the Congressman is powerless. He is powerless in this matter because the Seventy-third Congress abdicated its rightful power, delegated to it by the States and people in *Article 1, Section 8* of the Constitution.

The unemployed or displaced working man has no recourse. He must find another job, or sign up for "relief". Like corn or oats, his time is purchased and put in storage, perhaps to be offered later on the market at a bargain price.

When business, industry, farm or labor or citizens' organizations appear in Washington to protest, the word goes out and the publicity mill is put to work. The Nation is told that "selfish interests" again are pleading for "special treatment", and that these interests—citizens, like you and me—are interrupting the even tenor of "international cooperation"; to accede to their urgency would "increase inflation".*

The theory requires acceptance of a unique belief, and it is this: Support for anything international is described as not inflation; protection for anything at home is termed inflationary.

And what of the men and women on our farms? The several farm organizations can meet with representatives of the executive, and they do. They cannot say to that executive: "You listen to us and to our grievances, or we'll vote you out of office." No; they cannot say that. The executive's personnel are not voted into office. The executive with which farm organizations are obliged to treat is appointed—and often self-appointed—to its post.

It is a fact that farm organization after farm organization has re-

---

*PUBLISHER'S NOTE: This assertion by advocates of the policy is refuted by the facts. Using (only the) 1947 dollar as a base, the Department of Commerce in 1957 published its depreciating value over the past decade. This (1947) dollar depreciated $13,800,000,000 during the single year 1956. Its ten-year depreciation totalled $82,700,000,000. Here was the actual cost of the present policies—in price *inflation*.

peatedly gone on the record as opposed to farm subsidies in any form. The executive's publicity mill is silent on this fact. It is in opposition to the global theory.

Every farmer knows that certain agricultural products have been placed on an import-quota basis by the Government. Only so much cotton, grains, dairy products and peanuts may be imported into the United States in any single year. This is to "protect the home market", of course. But what do other nations—those other nations which are our friends, and which are so deeply imbued with the new era feeling for "international cooperation"—have to say to this? How do they react?

They react "in the spirit of GATT".

The "spirit of GATT" is illustrated by an article in the National City Bank (N. Y.) *Letter* for June 1955:

> At the Geneva conference this year to revise the 34-nation General Agreement on Tariffs and Trade (GATT), U. S. requests that member nations end quantitative restrictions on imports—particularly the discrimination against goods bought with dollars—caused delegates from other countries to point to U. S. import quotas on farm products as a case of the pot calling the kettle black.
>
> Whenever U. S. representatives pleaded for tighter regulations to reduce or eliminate the disruptive effect of governmental buying and selling of raw materials and manufactured products, other countries cited U. S. sales of butter and grain from CCC stocks. The president of Australia's National Farmers Union was quoted by a Geneva newspaper: "By her irresponsible disposal of agricultural surpluses, the U. S. is flagrantly breaking the spirit of GATT." Even more terse, the *Manchester* (England) *Guardian* pictured the United States as asking GATT for "legal permission to live in a state of sin."
>
> In an attempt to soften concern about possible dumping, the U. S. informed other GATT members that she was prepared to accept limits on her freedom to subsidize exports of farm products. While this was the first time in history the U. S. agreed to limitations of this kind, smaller countries, still fearful of competing with the U. S. Treasury in a subsidy war, apparently are skeptical.

Was this a mere instance? Was this the unfortunate remark of a diplomat who possibly had had a bad night?

Or was this expressive of the fundamental policy, of the basic articles of agreement, which is the charter itself of GATT?

Let us see.

The People of the United States are Permitted ...

My training as an engineer taught me at an early date the meticulous care which is required in calculating stresses and strains and torques. It also taught me the necessity for providing a "factor of safety", in any construction. The engineer is little interested in a structure's color or in its decorations, attractive as these may be. He is interested in the blueprint, and in the unseen factors which go into a construction. He is concerned, as you know, with stress and strain and torque.

As this book is read, it will be subjected to stress and strain and torque—to a great deal of it. Interested parties and organizations will attempt cleverly to divert you, and at times they may succeed. They will not take you into the blueprint room; they will not show you the foundations; they will not take you through the inside structure of this global economic world. You will be shown its color, and decorations; you will be shown its façade. You will be shown all that is most attractive.

To find out what goes on within the building one has almost to wire the place for sound. An elected representative of the people of these United States can report to you such essential matters only by dint of painstaking and concentrated work. And when you have before you the results, then you—citizen of the Republic—face no easy task. To bring this Government of ours back to proper citizen-control, it is essential that you demand that *your own representatives,* in this instance the Members of Congress, take back the Constitutional powers which have been abdicated. You can control the Congress.

The theory of executive rulership has gone so far that the citizens of this Republic are actually being permitted a course of action—*permitted,* if you please—by an international agency to which the power first abdicated to our own executive has been transferred.

The remarks at Geneva were not isolated remarks. They were remarks which are perfectly natural to a body which has itself received all but plenary power to act. Such power is fundamental to the charter of GATT.

On March 7, 1955, despatches from Geneva read:

The 34 nations of the General Agreement on Tariffs and Trade (GATT) have granted permission for the United States to continue to impose quantitative restrictions on certain agricultural products. But the members also gave other countries permission to retaliate and seek compensation if affected by the restrictions, which are contained in section 22 of the United States Agricultural Adjustment Act.

This section mainly concerns imports of dairy produce and had led to clashes with several nations in the past. Holland once retaliated by slashing imports of wheat from the United States. The United States is understood to have assured GATT that it will end any restrictions under the act as soon as they are no longer needed and consult with interested countries before taking further action.

If one discerned in this a subjugation of our farmers to the requirements of a foreign policy which was being internationally determined—and some discerned just that—the executive turned on the publicity mill and our people again were shown the glistening façade of the global structure which was being built.

Then GATT itself released the "decision" in a published report. This report received little publicity. There was no avalanche of editorials on the matter. The press was discreetly silent.

GATT's report was entitled *Decision to Grant a Waiver to the United States in Connection with Import Restrictions Imposed Under Section 22 of the United States Agricultural Adjustment Act (of 1933), as Amended.* The following is verbatim from that "decision":

1. Upon request of any contracting party which considers that its interests are seriously prejudiced by reason of any import restrictions imposed under section 22, whether or not covered by this decision, the United States will promptly undertake a review to determine whether there has been a change in circumstances which would require such restrictions to be modified or terminated. In the event the review shows a change, the United States will institute an investigation in the manner provided by section 22.

2. Should the President of the United States . . . . cause an investigation to be made . . . . the United States will notify the contracting parties and, in accordance with article XXIII of the general agreement, accord to any contracting party which considers that its interests would be prejudiced the fullest notice and opportunity, consistent with the legislative requirements of the United States, for representations and consultation.

4. As soon as the President has made his decision following any investigation the United States will notify the contracting parties . . . . [and] If the decision imposes restrictions on additional products or extends or intensifies existing restrictions the notification by the United States will include particulars of such restrictions and the reasons for them regardless of whether the restriction is consistent with the general agreement.

5. The United States will remove or relax each restriction permitted under this waiver as soon as it finds the circumstances requiring such restriction no longer exist or have changed so as no longer to require its imposition in its existing form.

6. The contracting parties will make an annual review of any action taken by the United States under this decision. For each such review the United States will furnish a report to the contracting parties showing .... the restrictions in effect under section 22 and the reasons why such restrictions (regardless of whether covered by this waiver) continue to be applied and any steps it has taken with a view to a solution of the problem of surpluses of agricultural commodities.

GATT states elsewhere in its "decision":

(a) To help solve the problem of surpluses . . . the United States Government has taken positive steps aimed at reducing 1955 crop supplies by lowering support levels or by imposing market quotas at minimum levels permitted by legislation; and that it is the intention of the United States Government to continue to seek a solution of the problem of surpluses of agricultural commodities.

(b) The assurance of the United States Government that it will discuss proposals under section 22 with all countries having a substantial interest prior to taking action, and will give prompt consideration to any representation made to it.

Here is the blueprint; here are the plans. Our Government signed the original blueprint and it agreed to the plans. Our "Government"? Not our *representative* Government. The Senate did not examine, weigh and debate the blueprint. The House did not examine, weigh and debate it.

Then how was the original blueprint designed and signed? It was designed and signed by the executive. GATT then was promulgated by the executive, in December 1947. Now, by this Geneva "decision", the Government of the United States would be required to do for *foreign* interests what that Government, by the Articles of its Constitution, was mandated to do for its own.

Upon business, upon shipping, industry and agriculture, and gradually upon every sector of our economy, the impact of this "decision" would fall.

The executive *alone* agreed to this procedure. Not one word of mine is needed to tell you that here, in GATT's "decision", is assumed a sovereignty which is as clear as it is simple and absolute.

By gracious waiver, this international authority permitted the United States of America a course of action. The permission was conditional, too, for report-cards must be submitted to the supreme authority.* The American farmer was voiceless and he was helpless. He was become a peasant, beholden to the program of an international authority which he can neither meet with nor control.

And what one authority—GATT—can do to farmers and growers it and other global authorities can do to industrialists, to steamship operators, to men of business. They have no recourse. They may plead with the local executive, to be sure. The local executive is resident in Washington, D. C. But that executive, in turn, must plead with an international authority. It must plead with a supplicant's voice.

The people of this Nation? They have no voice at all. They are to consider themselves "citizens of the world".

For the World, a "New Era" — for America, "A New Social Order"

In education, in politics and in economics there emerges the evidence of a plan, seemingly coordinated, to mold into a "new order" all of human endeavor. Its documentation to the contrary notwithstanding, all evidence is met with denial. The evidence mounts.

The painstaking work of *documenting* this evidence has been undertaken by many people, and very often it has entailed sacrifices which are considerable. Evidence of the existence of a plan has been separately offered and documented in the fields of education, of politics and of economics. Evidence has begun to appear in the fields of science and of sociology. Like all true research, the work has required the utmost concentration.

In their essential concentration, few people as yet have had the time or the resources to discover that—plan or no plan—there is mounting evidence of coordination. The program whose impact strikes first at education, strikes later and inevitably at politics and at our economy. Where the impact is first felt in politics—as in the Status of Forces agreement—it strikes later and inevitably in the fields of economics and of

*The first report-card was submitted in November 1955. The measures adopted pursuant to its obligations were listed in detail, and the American executive hoped the supreme authority would agree that it was "moving in the right direction".

education. Where the impact is at first in economics—as with the Trade Agreements Act—later, inevitably, the impact strikes in our schools and in the business world.

There is to be observed another phenomenon, and it is this: The personalities, and the organizations who and which defend the program in one field, are found to be the very personalities and organizations who and which defend *other* programs in the other fields. They are the same personalities and organizations who and which decry, even besmirch and smear, their fellow-citizens who are exercising the God-given right of individual judgment and action in actively opposing a plan of whose existence they are convinced.

In our schools, interested persons and organizations are promoting a theory which way back in 1933 stated that—and this highly significant statement is *not* "lifted out of context"—

the school can scarcely hope to function effectively until society is already transformed . . . . *

Sixteen years later, UNESCO—an agency of the world *political* organization—set forth its own, universal, development of that theory, and stated that

To fulfil such expectations it is clear that everything in the world would have to be changed . . . . *

It is denied that there is any connection whatsoever between the educational program and the political developments. Yet at least one nationwide education association openly states that there *is*

an intimate connection between the domestic effort to achieve a more socialized economy and the world effort to develop a democratic system of collective security.*

Whatever their merits or demerits, certain it is that a number of programs—whether separate or coordinated—are taking place; that their advocates receive widespread audiences in our schools; that the writings which propound them are quickly installed as texts and as, "recommended reading"; that influential book reviews are given over almost exclusively to them; and that no avenue of publicity is overlooked in their promotion.

It is equally certain that the views of other citizens whose studies lead them to raise their voices—and in however scholarly a fashion—in exami-

---

The Turning of the Tides: Hon. Paul W. Shafer and John Howland Snow. THE LONG HOUSE, INC. New York; 1953, 1956 (pp. 149-50).

nation of or in objection to the several programs, find no such ready, receptive channels of free discussion, and no comparable underwriting for their research and distribution. This is demonstrably true, from school assembly lectures to teacher-appointments; in men's and women's clubs; and with radio, TV and newspaper and magazine reviews. "Academic freedom", in other words, is ever-present—if the views expressed do not diverge from those whose interest it is to promote them.

This book is primarily devoted to the *economic* impact of the pincers. The impact upon our business life can be felt, and seen. Limited as my political and educational references perforce must be, justice would not be done were it not stressed that the pincers movement is all-embracing, and that all of us are its victims—accidental or intended.

Within its compass, under the cloak of "collective security", there is now developing a pattern which is not merely dangerous to our safety as a Nation; it could be fatal. This pattern concerns materials of vital military and strategic importance. Some of their sources are in our own back yard; some are in the Western Hemisphere; others are more distant.

The very essence of militarily strategic materials is their availability. Further, I believe that you will agree that, for our own Nation's security, we are perfectly willing to pay higher prices for such materials in order to assure their ready access in time of true emergency.

The opposite course is being pursued.

Mica, for instance, was flown in under top priority, from India, during the second world war. Why didn't we mine our own mica? That did not suit the "new era" policy. Under that policy we are becoming increasingly, and alarmingly, dependent upon distant sources for such vital materials as uranium, manganese, industrial diamonds, tin and columbium. During the war, under War Production Board Order *L-208,* we shut down our gold mines. Gold mines, however, continued in operation abroad. We made mining machinery and exported it, to keep foreign gold mines in operation. Naturally, our mines flooded. Miners went into other occupations. Such metals as silver, lead and zinc were soon in short supply. We began to purchase them elsewhere. This pattern has been developed to such an extent that in the event of conflict we could be almost entirely dependent upon distant sources for many of our most vital materials of war. Our ships would be forced to sail over thousands of miles of submarine and airplane infested waters, and our seamen would be forced to man them. The situation is so fraught with clear and present danger that a committee of the United States Senate made it the object of an intensive investigation.

The Minerals, Metals and Fuels Economics Subcommittee of the Senate Committee on Interior and Insular Affairs undertook the task. Its report was published July 9, 1954 as *Senate Report 1627*, and is available from the Government Printing Office at Washington. The *Report* fills 415 pages, including the index. It summarizes 10 published volumes of evidence, secured through 58 hearings which extended over a period of ten months. The Subcommittee had the assistance of some of America's most able industrial and military men. Its *Report*, in the strongest possible terms, recommended a total shift in our strategic materials policy. It recommended a shift to American producers, and to producers in the Western Hemisphere. It recommended the normal, natural and understandable policy of basing our Nation's defense potential upon materials sources which would be as safe for us as possible, as close to us as possible, and as far removed as could be from potential enemy control. It said:

> The Committee determined that the Western Hemisphere can be defended and that it will be the only "dependable" source of the necessary critical materials during any all-out world war.
>
> . . . . .
>
> The advent of the long-range sonic speed bomber and fighter planes, guided missiles, radar control, and nuclear-powered submarines, through the use of new and improved materials including uranium, titanium, columbium, thorium, zirconium, and tantalum has strengthened the defensive and offensive position of the Western Hemisphere.

To all intents and purposes, the executive ignored this *Report*. The findings lent neither credence nor assurance to the theory by which the executive was obsessed.

Neither the political nor the economic programs pursued since the adoption of the Trade Agreements Act of 1934 have strengthened the defensive position of the Western Hemisphere. The policy which has placed more and more American ships under foreign flags—and 30,000 of our own seamen "on the beach"—has not strengthened our own defensive position at sea. The policy which flooded mines and put our own miners out of work, has not strengthened our defensive position. The policy is making us—and the entire Western Hemisphere—steadily and increasingly more dependent upon distant sources for critical war materials. Foreign sources which can stop—as they have stopped—the shipment of monazite sands (used in atomic fission) to us in time of peace, can stop the shipment of *any* critical material in time of war.

The program completely disregards the natural common interests which could bind in growing cooperation the peoples of the two great continents of the Western Hemisphere. Yet real concern is being voiced by responsible sources among the very ones who are closest to us, our good neighbors to the north with whom we have the longest undefended frontier known to history.

Canada's tourists are spending each year a hundred million dollars more in the United States than our folks spend in travel there. Her trade with us amounts to 59 percent of all her foreign business. She purchases more agricultural products from us than we do from her, by over a hundred million dollars each year. She buys several times more of our exports than does our second-best customer, and the amount is increasing. She buys one-quarter of all our exports. Her American purchases during 1954-5 equalled those of all of western Europe combined — though Europe has sixteen times her population.

The descriptions we hear of our foreign trade become somewhat less impressive when we take into consideration these shipments to our own next-door neighbor. Moreover, our policies have been hurting this natural and valued friend. They have contributed materially to the largest trade-deficit in Canadian history, and responsible citizens there are observing—with truth—that in regard to Canada's greatest single export commodity, wheat, they seem to be holding a price umbrella over our practices of surplus-disposal. "How", they observe, "can we compete? Who will buy our huge accumulation when wheat can be had for the asking, or for local currencies which then remain in the countries of purchase?" Canadians are also concerned lest a revision upward of our tariffs not seriously affect their lead and zinc mines, their fishing and lumber industries, and their growing petroleum trade. (Canada is presently a net importer of American oil.)

A concept of Western Hemisphere defense, including its natural communality of economic interests, would take these things into consideration, and I believe they should be taken into consideration. Militarily, the Western Hemisphere can be defended, as *Senate Report 1627* (83/2) made exhaustively clear. Economically, a flexible tariff could not only accomplish the reasonable objectives of commerce and trade, it would be fair to our natural friends and honorably retain their friendship.

GATT is an international authority superimposed over our own representative Government. And GATT, if designed for the purpose, could not be a more effective means to make our Nation progressively, then all but completely, dependent upon foreign sources for our defense and war-making potential.

That is the hard cold fact.

At its base is stark military necessity. And the final assessment is this: If we are attacked, do we survive or perish?

The political arm of the pincers, as I have said, is the more open, the more sensational. As our citizens awaken to the peril, they may well succeed in freeing us of it. We will then be confronted with the ultimate force, and this is economic. And we will find that it has bound us *strategically* to "the new world order"; we will have been bereft of strength. In defense, we will be impotent.

Here is the ultimate impact of its force and pressure.

Freed from the one, we will find ourselves inextricably bound by the other. For the ultimate in its pressure is this: By following a global theory, *we will have surrendered all reasonably direct access to the critical materials upon which our military strength is based.*

That is the importance of our recognizing the dual program, the political and the economic, and the global theory which is at its base.

Industry, Finance and Employment in the Global Market-Place

Cordell Hull had not always entertained the ideas which were embodied in the Trade Agreements Act which he sponsored. He was one of many men whose views altered materially upon becoming a member of the executive branch, even at Cabinet level.

In 1955 Congress considered a bill designated as *H.R. 1*. Among its purposes, this bill was designed "to extend the authority of the President to enter into trade agreements under section 350 of the Tariff Act of 1930." Now, the Tariff Act of 1930 provided for a flexible tariff. When that Act was before Congress, Mr. Hull was a member of the House Ways and Means Committee. This was long before Congress was "reorganized"; Ways and Means was not only an important Committee, it was extremely powerful. What were Mr. Hull's views on those provisions in the 1930 Tariff Act which enlarged the executive authority? They are on record in his minority report. Mr. Hull called those provisions "subversive of the plain functions of Congress."

Mr. Hull continued to refer to the 1930 bill as an "unjustifiable arrogance of power and authority to the President." On May 9, 1932 Cordell Hull said that these provisions virtually vested in the President "supreme taxing powers of the Nation, contrary to the plainest and most fundamental provisions of the Constitution."

I agree with those statements.

The Trade Agreements Act was passed by the Seventy-third Congress in 1934. Ten Acts passed by that Congress subsequently were declared unconstitutional by the Supreme Court. No other Congress has achieved such an ignominious record. The Trade Agreements Act has not come before the Supreme Court.

After twenty-two years, the practice of shifting Congressional responsibilities to the executive (titularly, to the President) whenever he so demands, has become ominously habitual. In some cases responsibility has been merely delegated; in the Trade Agreements Act the *Constitutional* responsibility was abdicated.

By its acquiescence in the terms of that Act, the Congress set industry upon industry; and it set groups of workingmen against other groups of workingmen, all in a mad scramble to survive. Each man tried to save himself from extinction. Each urged that his own product or group be taken care of by provision or by dispensation; each was obliged to ignore the impact of his own interest upon all others; none, it seemed, could afford recognition that the impact upon each separate one was cumulative, that it would come to vitally affect the Nation as a whole.

Few were able even to make an attempt to get together, in order to avert the mass-sacrifice which was yet to come. This mass-sacrifice was to be offered by the proponents of the theory of One Economic World, on the altar of their distant idol.

The executive took over in 1934. No factual compilation of statistics can successfully prove that what the executive did during the next ensuing years advanced the permanent welfare of the people of this Country. Then came war, and unemployment disappeared. The planners were off the hook. The Nation, properly, forgot everything but "Let's get it over with."

Now we are beginning to discover what has been going on, in education, in politics, and in the realm of economics. We find our Constitution amended by executive decree, by legislative act and by judicial fiat. We find our laws and our governance subordinated to interpretations which must be consistent with "the purposes and principles of the United Nations". We find our business, our shipping, our trade, our working men and women being subjected to "waivers", permits and mandates of international "authorities".

We find that, in the fight for survival, even American businesses are going abroad, and that the Government is "granting" to them overseas protection, granting returns on their investments, and actually extending preferred treatment inimical to our own working citizens, by preferential tariffs on articles which are thus being manufactured abroad and imported here, to compete with the employment of our own men and women. In January 1957 the International Cooperation Administration (ICA) added insurance against possible war damage to these plants. The premium was set at ½ percent per year, and the maximum coverage at 90 percent of the dollar investment.

Again a very different policy is being followed here at home. In the train of war and inflation is the mounting fact of *debt*. Much of our seeming prosperity rests upon that debt. It is directly traceable to the policies of the last six administrations, followed without deviation by the one presently in office. Let me illustrate.

More than 85 percent of the taxes collected by the Federal Government come from individual and corporate income levies. An individual is permitted certain deductions before taxes, and these deductions may loosely be compared to the operating expenses of industry. The individual is also permitted to "write off" certain sums expended on his home, in case of sale. This write-off may (very loosely) be compared to industry's Reserve for Depreciation and Replacement. Here the comparison ends, for industry must *constantly* replace its productive plant. The rates at which this replacement may be amortized are fixed arbitrarily by the Government and two serious fallacies are employed in the process. First, the Reserve is permitted only to the amount of the plant's original dollar-cost; and second, a constant value of the dollar is assumed. The first fallacy permits a Reserve of $1 original cost to replace equipment now priced at $1.43 and up; the second freezes a *new* Reserve at the equipment's dollar-cost when the dollar is depreciating at a rate approximating 3% a year. Industry's allowable Reserves thus fall far short of the sums necessary for plant replacement.

How, then, is industry replacing its obsolete or worn-out equipment? It is doing exactly what a private individual would do. It is going into debt. The private citizen does so of his own free will. Illness or disaster may overtake him, to be sure; but such unfortunate situations have behind them no human force or plan. With industry the matter is entirely different; there is nothing voluntary about it. Industry is *forced* to borrow, and in the face of the greatest era of seeming prosperity ever known. Industry is borrowing at a rate of some $30,000,000,000 a year, even as it shows a ratio of "profits" which evokes the condemnation of its ideological detractors. Fully a third of this borrowing (half of the declared "profits") would be eliminated by proper, established accounting practice. Funds normally and correctly set aside to Reserve accounts are thus—and by governmental dictum—automatically channeled into Profit, and the billions so channeled are themselves subjected to the 52 percent tax on corporate earnings. The tax on such funds is a tax on debt. An average of 60 percent of industry's profits is distributed to stockholders, and the latter are receiving dividends against six to eight billion dollars which annually are declared as "profits" instead of being set aside into Reserves. To the last penny that these sums are subsequently borrowed for re-tooling, stockholders are receiving dividends against debt. This creates an entirely exaggerated picture of industry's true position, and it is building up a situation which some day can bring economic disaster to us all.

Corporate executives are perfectly aware that an industry which does not provide for constant replacement is an industry which is doomed. And they are acutely conscious of the fact that the tax structure, made obligatory by our global policies, *is forcing them to declare profits which do not exist.* These policies are forcing industry—as they are forcing local, State and national governments—to hypothecate the future for the semblance of present "prosperity." The recorded indebtedness in the private sector passed $400,000,000,000 by the end of 1956, and it is rising. It is a material factor in the general inflation.

That is why, for the moment, "You never had it so good." It is also a main reason for the difficulties which face tens of thousands of small businesses.

The economy of our Nation is being traded in the market place, in pursuance of a political theory which, we are told, is a "foreign policy for peace"—and the executive is remaking the industrial map of our own Country in pursuit of the chimera. The executive has been acting on this premise since 1934. The "Democrats" started it. The "Republicans" have continued and accelerated it. The citizens of the Republic have had no voice in the matter at all. And they will have no voice in the matter until they—through their elected representatives—take back from the executive every vestige of the Constitutional legislative power which the executive has now assumed.

The Founders of this Nation had been so pushed around by distant kings and by local colonial dictators (called Governors) that they drew up the Articles of our Constitution in such a way as to estop forever a reversion to such colonialism. No one dreamed that the representatives of a sovereign people would some day voluntarily revert to such a status, and that they would abdicate the very power which had been delegated to them in order to prevent it.

But they did.

The citizens of this Nation must require them to take it back.

Can you blame an American company for building a plant overseas, for making products there, for then shipping those products back and selling them on this market? It seems to me that that is human nature. Can you blame men and women, technicians, for accepting lucrative positions to train and supervise workers abroad? That is human nature. And if in the process a nation is to suffer, if it is to find itself in strategic jeopardy, who of us would refuse such employ, when a thousand others will jump at the jobs?

Were these facts the (at times painful) hazards of evolution, of the ever-changing pattern of economic life, or of new technology or of new discoveries, the scope of our concern would be more circumscribed. They are none of these. They result from the application of a theory, a belief, a *mystique*. As long ago as July 12, 1949 I quoted the then Secretary of State, Dean Acheson, who made the following declaration:

> It is hardly possible any longer to draw a sharp dividing line between the economic affairs and the political affairs. Each compliments and supplements the other. They must be combined in a single unified and rounded policy.

Has Congress made this "single unified and rounded policy"? Did our citizens make it? Were they even asked if they acquiesced in it? Or has an "unjustifiable arrogance of power and authority" to the executive been the one great factor?

It is this "single unified and rounded policy" which is the *mystique*. And is it bringing peace? Yes—of a sort. We had 23 years of peace between 1918 and 1941. We had five years of peace between 1945 and 1950. We have had some peace since Korea. And what has been that peace? It has been, and is, an era of perpetual war. The war itself is for peace, of course.

And that is the executive policy. Others have defined it. The policy is perpetual war, for perpetual peace.

Korea was political war, by executive decree.

GATT is economic war—by executive decree.

Contrast

I have no desire to be understood as suggesting that our Country withdraw into a political or economic shell; nor do I point with scorn at foreign spokesmen who make the best bargains they can with the Government or traders of the United States. On the contrary, I take my hat off to them. I think our traders should trade with anyone they wish, and determine—each one for himself—what constitutes profitable trade.

What is at fault is the overall policy, the theory itself. Because of that, I cannot find it possible to censure anyone for moving machinery, or abilities, behind a low-wage curtain and shipping the resultant products here. But it ill becomes a Congressional and executive procedure which makes such moves possible, even unavoidable, inevitable.

The citizens of this Nation cannot control the executive—but they *can* control the Congress. That is the essence of the matter.

The executive is handing out the taxpayers' money in pursuit of a theory little short of incredible. It is like a groceryman who finds business a little slack and borrows money from a bank; then he throws the money around the neighborhood and hopes that some of it will come back to him in trade. Trade, he may have. But the grocer will remain delicately reticent should you ask him point-blank if his accounts are showing him a *profit*.

The Trade Agreements Act of 1934 was passed as an "emergency measure". It was to last three years. Three years went by. The date of expiration approached. The executive turned on the publicity mill; it molded leadership opinion, and it pressured Congress. Every word and gesture was designed to foster the conviction that "just one more" extension would bring about the results originally proclaimed. That has been the procedure ever since, as each succeeding renewal-period approached its end. In 1955 the Act was extended for three more years.

In 1955, mounting opposition to the program resulted in several variations. On paper, these provisions appeared to afford relief. They included: (*1*) A requirement that the President report annually to Congress on any new negotiations or modifications which affected existing trade agreements; (*2*) a requirement that the Tariff Commission report on the effects upon the United States of foreign duties and import restrictions and that it publish both its majority and dissenting findings, opinions and recommendations; (*3*) a requirement that the Commission consider an industry to be threatened by our tariff reductions if the latter "contribute substantially" to the threat; and (*4*) the President was empowered to limit imports of any article if and when he found that its import had become a threat to national defense.

These were concessions to our own citizens, by our own Government.

A dependent citizenry received them from a benign executive, as once their colonial forebears had received concessions from a kindhearted representative of the Crown. Empire-limited had been that authority of two hundred years ago; now there has emerged a vaster pattern, global in awesome contrast. The contrast was personified by GATT.

GATT altered completely the stated purposes of Cordell Hull's program. The change was basic. The "trade agreements" of that program were bilateral, and they resembled treaties. Agreements now are multilateral, and determined by international directorates. The American executive already is functioning by "waiver" and by "permission".

The 1934 Act was to benefit "agriculture, industry, mining and commerce"; it was "for the purpose of expanding foreign markets for the products of the United States." It was an "emergency" measure, to last three years. When the Act was again extended in 1955, the purpose still was to expand the foreign markets of our products and for "establishing and maintaining a better relationship among various branches of American agriculture, industry, mining and commerce." After twenty-two years there still is not one statutory word in behalf of domestic producers for the domestic market of these United States. Of the plethora of verbal assurances which you have heard, not one is mandatory in the bills.

Let me now outline, briefly and for the record, a part of the maze of executive-appointed groups which led us deviously but unerringly to our present situation.

Between 1934 and 1947, there were negotiated 29 bilateral trade agreements, of which 27 were in force. Then, on December 16, 1947 the President declared the General Agreement on Tariffs and Trade in effect as of January 1, 1948. The bilateral principle was abandoned. Trade agreements became multilateral overnight. The President claimed the Act of 1934 as the source of his authority for the decree.

GATT, as we have seen, evolved outside of these United States. Within our Nation, the GATT developed as follows. On December 22, 1941 an Advisory Committee on Postwar Foreign Policy was set up. This Committee had subcommittees on "economic policy" and on "economic reconstruction". On April 9, 1943 the Committee was dissolved, and the Committee on Postwar Foreign Economic Policy was organized. Dean Acheson, then Assistant Secretary of State, was given "general supervision" of the following sectors of our economy: "Shipping, relaxation of trade barriers, commodity agreements and methods of trade, private monopolies and cartels, food and agricultural products, metals and heavy industries, petroleum, and rubber." Meanwhile our men overseas went about their grim business of winning the war.

On November 23, 1944 Mr. Acheson announced the official intention of his Department. The intention was "to seek an early understanding with the leading trading nations, indeed as many nations as possible, for the effective and substantial reduction of all kinds of barriers to trade." The words were alluring, and he added: " . . . . a trade conference of the United and Associated Nations should be held at the earliest practicable date for the negotiation of an agreement for the reduction of all kinds of barriers to trade."

The Assistant Secretary added further: "This agreement would of course be submitted to the Congress for its consideration." What was submitted was the charter of the ITO. The ITO charter was so inimical to American interests that it wasn't even reported out of committee.

GATT was not submitted at all. It was announced by executive decree.

Earlier, on April 5, 1944, the President created another committee, the Executive Committee on Economic Foreign Policy. For years, this Committee was the main organ before which were brought the key economic and cultural (social) problems for interdepartmental consideration and coordination. Dean Acheson, Harry Dexter White and Lauchlin Currie were original members of this committee. A Special Committee on Relaxation of Trade Barriers was created, and on it White also served.* Alger Hiss sat on a Special Committee on Petroleum. An interdivisional committee on problems of overall economic organization was formed, "at the expert level". The chairman of this Committee was Leo Pasvolsky, and Charles P. Taft was a member. The Committee was " . . . . concerned with the formulation of proposals for permanent economic organization to accompany those being developed in the political field for the maintenance of peace and security." This Committee "functioned during the spring of 1944 within the [State] Department's preparatory structure, its work being absorbed in June by the Group preparing for the Dumbarton Oaks Conversations."

During this period, and while the economic pattern was being steadily set forth, similar activity was being carried on in the political field. An Advisory Committee on Post-War Foreign Policy was suggested by the Department of State, and the suggestion was approved by the President in late December, 1941. With varying personnel, this Advisory Committee continued its activities over the years. Among its initial membership were

---

*White was also one of the key figures in setting up the World Bank.

Isaiah Bowman, James T. Shotwell, Mrs. Anne O'Hare McCormick, Walter P. Reuther, Brooks Emeny, Benjamin Cohen, David K. Niles and Leo Pasvolsky.

Here, barely three weeks after Pearl Harbor, was emerging the pattern of the eventual pincers move. Two years later appeared the slogan on its velvet wrapping. The words were "peace and security".

It was the Acheson-White-Currie committee, organized on April 5, 1944 which submitted the document entitled *Proposals for the Expansion of World Trade and Employment* to which reference has been made. Participating in the preparation of this document were three representatives of the Treasury: Harry Dexter White, V. Frank Coe and Harold Glasser. This document (as has been seen) was the forerunner of GATT.

On December 15, 1945 the executive branch announced its plans for an international conference on trade and employment. In February 1946 UNESCO undertook to sponsor the conference and set up a preparatory committee for the purpose. Harold Glasser, V. Frank Coe and Victor Perlo, all of the Treasury Department, were members of this preparatory committee. The conference was held in London during October 1946. Here were recommended the procedures designed to give effect "to certain provisions of the charter of the International Trade Organization by means of a General Agreement on Tariffs and Trade."

The Geneva Conference was next, and it met from April to October 1947. It was part of the second session of the preparatory committee for a United Nations Conference on Trade and Employment. Here, GATT was born. On December 16, GATT was given its birth certificate in the United States. The fact was announced by Presidential proclamation.

It is claimed that the General Agreement on Tariffs and Trade is "reciprocal". This simply is not true. Every beneficial clause in its charter is negated by a further clause which "excepts" the benefits previously proclaimed. The charter of GATT presents to prosperous nations a series of high-sounding phrases; it immediately exempts from their terms any nation which it determines is less than prosperous. Under *Art. XI* no restrictions other than "duties, taxes, or other charges, whether made effective through quotas, import or export licenses or other measures, shall be instituted or maintained by any contracting party on the importation of any product of the territory" of another member. *Art. XIII* immediately enumerates GATT's exceptions: Any member may "restrict the quantity or value of merchandise permitted to be imported" whenever it wishes to "safeguard its external financial position and balance of payments." And which nations have that terrible incubus, a "dollar-shortage"? Why, every other trading nation in the world except our own. Should any nation come to enjoy a favorable balance of payments, it becomes *ipso facto* subject to the rules which in this charter apply, with singular exclusivity, to us.

Thus GATT is a leveler of all nations. It applies to every one of them the dictum: "From each according to his abilities; to each according to his needs."

GATT emerges also as a global structure erected on behalf of debtors. The United States is the one great "creditor" nation—albeit our "credit" is now based on debt.

"Reciprocity"? When *H.R. 1* was before the Congress—the bill which in 1955 extended the Trade Agreements Act for three more years—the Senate Finance Committee heard testimony that 32 nations favored tariff cuts on goods which they exported to the United States. Every one of these nations had recently increased its tariffs on American goods. Not one of them—not any nation, for that matter—imposed the tariffs for the only admissable business reason there is, namely, to equalize the wage-standards of living between two countries engaged in trade.

"Reciprocity"? Of 91 trading nations, 68 at that time were requiring import licenses on American goods generally; 9 others required licenses on some of our products; 10 others linked exchange permits to import licenses. Only ten nations applied no control regulations at all on imports of American goods.

The Executive Pincers — and Representative Government

Over 55,000 concessions have now been made, all of them to freeze or lower America's tariffs. An average reduction of 68 percent is now in effect, and our tariffs are the lowest of any major trading nation in the world. When *H.R. 1* was before Congress in 1955, despite the claims of "international cooperation", every one of the following nations had but recently raised its tariffs against American products: *Australia, Belgium,* Bolivia, *Brazil, Ceylon,* Costa Rica, *Cuba, Denmark, Dominican Republic,* Ecuador, Egypt, *Finland, France, Guatemala, Haiti, India,* Jordan, Lebanon, Mexico, *New Zealand, Norway, Peru, Sweden,* Syria, Thailand, *Union of South Africa, United Kingdom, Uruguay* and West Germany.

The United States had trade agreements with every country listed in *italics,* and all of them except Guatemala were covered by trade agreements made through GATT. Thus specifically, GATT is shown to mean free trade for the United States; protection for everyone else—

until all nations shall be brought to a common level, in one economic world.

Those of us who oppose the program have been labeled everything from "Isolationists" to "Inhumanitarians". Yet our predictions are coming true. I myself predicted that the 1934 Act would ultimately result in the centralized control of our domestic trade and commerce and transportation; the centralized control of farmers and of agriculture. I predicted that for their own salvation whole industries would be forced to go abroad; that other industries, and entire communities, would be closed down and bodily "relocated" within these United States. In portentous part, the predictions have been fulfilled. Their further fulfillment is in process.

In the matter of national survival the situation is in fact ominous. When Harry Dexter White was Assistant Secretary of the Treasury, he sent a memorandum to his superior in office, Henry Morgenthau. This memorandum stated that we were about to run out of many of our most critical and strategic materials, naming petroleum, manganese, tungsten and seven or eight others. Therefore, said the White memorandum, we should conserve what we had; we should lend enough money to the U.S.S.R. so the U.S.S.R. could produce them for us. (White wrote two letters; one suggested an advance of $5,000,000,000 and the other suggested $10,000,000,000.)

Morgenthau prepared a letter to the President. This letter contained almost the same verbiage as had the White memorandum. Then one day the President announced that it was the policy of the United States to conserve its crucial materials and to import as much as we could from overseas.

This announcement was immediately interpreted abroad as revealing that we had become a "have-not" nation. How else could the announcement have been interpreted? Clearly, if we were obliged to import our most vital materials we could no longer sustain a major military campaign. The possibility which this opened up can be expressed in plain words: The United States from that moment could be subjected to blackmail in time of peace, and to potential destruction in time of war.

One "escape" was left open to us: We could join with others in "One Economic World." We could make free to others our markets, our resources, our immigration—and take our chances on the result.

Under *Art. XXIII* of GATT, and under *Arts. III, XV* and *XXIII* of its judicial counterpart, the OTC, the position of our Country is just that.

Our entire fiscal and economic policy becomes subordinate to "international authority".*

Already a coalition of 34 nations has been put in a position to control the agriculture and industry of the United States and to utterly ignore the powers and responsibilities delegated to Congress by *Article 1, Section 8* of the Constitution.

Ten members of the House Ways and Means Committee are on the record as foreseeing such eventualities as far back as 1934. When that Committee considered the Trade Agreements Act, these ten men (of a total Committee of 25) submitted their minority report. This report flatly declared the Act to be not only unconstitutional, but un-American.

I fully subscribe to that view.

Like other phenomena which directly and intimately concern our people, this phase of the overall pattern is not revealed by the publicity mill. These facts are not included in the material which is offered to writers, columnists and historians—and many publishers ignore them or deny them when they are presented in manuscript form. Our citizens, you see, must continue to have unblemished faith in "international co-operation", and in the "collective security" which is ushering in for us the "new era". Our Country must be a "partner" in the new Organization for Trade Cooperation (OTC).

And what is the OTC? It is the executive's new counterpart of the defunct ITO. It is a further authority, another development of GATT. It is part of the program.

" . . . . each part of this program is important", said an Assistant Secretary of State in 1949, "Each contributes to an effective and consistent whole."†

In 1934, the legitimate foreign trade—trade for which the shipper looked for payment to other traders, not to the American taxpayer—amounted to between 4½ and 5½ percent of our total trade. This ratio had been maintained for something like fifty years. Now, after more than two decades of the "new" theory, after twenty-two years of "emergency", of "international cooperation" and of "collective security", the ratio of legitimate trade—for which the supplier is paid by customers, not by the taxpayer—is between 4½ and 5½ percent.

The global theory has *not* increased legitimate foreign trade.

The United States exported 12.9% of its production of movable goods in 1921; 9.1% in 1923; 10.1% in 1925; 9.9% in 1927; 9.6% in 1929;

Basic Instruments and Selected Documents (Vol. II, p. 115).
†Willard L. Thorpe, testifying on the ITO on January 24, 1949.

7.3% in 1931; 6.5% in 1933 (depression years). This trade was legitimate; it was a normal, private business venture. Foreign "aid" had not then been invented.

Excluding the war years, and excluding exports financed solely by the taxpayers, exports since 1946 show the following percentages of our total production of movable goods: 4.9%, 7.3%, 5.4%, 4.8%, 4.1%, 6.2%, 5.8%, 5.1% and 6.0%.

Application of the theory has not increased legitimate foreign trade in movable goods.

Legitimate exports have not increased; imports have steadily risen. On the other hand, the policy has created an atmosphere so favorable for the export of American capital that the income from its foreign investment equalled, in 1955, the entire sum of new (American) lending. In some overseas areas the American supervisory personnel of machine and factory operators was as high as ten percent. In Britain, American subsidiaries and jointly owned Anglo-American factories produced in 1954 alone some £550 million ($1,540,000,000 at $2.80 the £) worth of American-styled and designed goods. Probably half as much again was turned out by British firms manufacturing under American licenses. Nearly four-fifths of the "American products" bought by British consumers were actually manufactured in the United Kingdom.*

In certain engineering and chemical lines, the United Kingdom had become almost self-sufficient. Yet as recently as 1938 Britain had obtained almost 70 percent of its requirements from outside the British Isles, usually from the United States. British exports in these classifications, 3% of the corresponding United States exports in 1938, had risen to 40% by 1954. British exports of washing machines, refrigerators, farm tractors and excavating equipment just about equalled those of the United States.

"Reciprocity"? "Freeing world trade"? "Non-discrimination"? This surge of British trade was aided by H. M. Government's official "foreign market restrictions against dollar products, which have provided an incentive for manufacturing in the United Kingdom and selling for sterling. Another factor has been the difference between U. S. and U. K. wage costs† and the steady increase in the comparative efficiency of U. K.

---

*The total of all American investments in foreign countries was some $26,500,000,000; it had earned some $2,500,000,000 in returns by the end of 1954. During 1955 investment rose by $2.4 billion and in 1956 by $3.9 billion, to a total of $32,977,000,000.

†Top workers' wages in 1955 in Britain were: Auto workers, $38.02 per week; air transport repairmen, $35.90; aircraft manufacture and repairmen, $35.73; iron and steel smelting and rolling, $35.30. Coal miners and dock workers averaged $36.29. For *all* workers, the average was $25.50. Men averaged $30.41; women averaged $15.71; boys averaged $12.67; girls averaged $9.98. The average working week for these wages was 48.9 hours. (The dollar figures are at $2.80 the £.) Source: *Industrial News.* Trades Union Congress, London. October 14, 1955.

subsidiaries aided by U. S. research and development; many of these firms are now manufacturing at costs from one third to one half those of the parent U. S. companies."†

Thus the British have been taking care of their own. Thus the global theory is siphoning off America's wealth and bringing her economy to the level of others'. Thus the theory is displacing American workers who otherwise would be employed. The office force, sales force, and the suppliers of American plants all suffer. And the policy of the United States executive is to protect the investment which is made abroad, to guarantee it against political risks, to guarantee its returns, to favor its products by tariff dispensation, and to grant to it tax deductions and rates of amortization which heretofore they have never enjoyed and to which they are not entitled.

Every move of this procedure is against the normal, proper interests of the Country which the executive is sworn to represent.

In 1934 the President stated that "no sound and important American interest will be injuriously disturbed" by the passage of the Trade Agreements Act.‡ After twenty-two years we find that the legislation has not only enabled the executive to "injuriously disturb" industry and agriculture but to severely damage and in part to destroy both. The policy is contrary to every statutory tradition of the Republic. On the surface, it has helped bring prosperity. And this seeming prosperity has stemmed from trade artificially stimulated by foreign wars and by the preparation for further foreign wars. It is now based upon a continuing war economy induced by threats of still further wars—while its proponents and its trusting advocates cry "Peace". It has been promoted and expanded by recurrent and executive-enlarged emergencies which, one after the other, have taken from our people in gifts and grants to foreign political authorities more than one hundred billion dollars; and it has subjected the people and their elected Congress to foreign and domestic propaganda which links our giveaway trade and taxes to fears of ideological aggression.

It is building an executive authority in our Nation which is the structural counterpart of the Total State which the theory is alleged to be designed to "combat".   It is erecting an international executive authority which differs from a world socialist government only in the open candor with which the latter's advocates espouse their goal.

Abdication of the legislative power by the very instrument created

†*District Bank Review,* Manchester, England. September, 1955.
‡*Senate Report 232.* Eighty-fourth Congress, First Session. 1955.

by the Constitution—the Congress—has handed to the executive a potential dictatorship over the people and their sovereign States. The executive
has set out upon a global program geared not to peace but to an economy
of permanent war. The program stifles normal trade relations in time of
peace, by attempting to purchase "security" through the progressive
sacrifice of the living standards of our people. Its theory is subjecting our
economy to the unconscionable manipulation of an international executive cartel. It subjects world trade to the direction of centralized governments which include monarchies, "democracies", and socialist and communist dictatorships—none of which, like ours, is truly representative
in its basic structure; all of which are built upon the ancient theory of
Power-in-the-State.

By so doing, it, the United States executive, has brought about what
the late, great Garet Garrett called a *revolution within the form*. The
executive branch has turned back the clock of human history a hundred
and seventy-five years. Its guiding concept has become increasingly similar
to that of political authorities abroad, old-fashioned, socialist, and reactionary. It is participating in a movement whose result can only be the
international socialist dictatorship of the world.

In form, the Republic remains.

People are told that this is all being done in the interest of a "foreign
policy for peace".

This is not the haven which we were promised as desperately we
sought a right course in the fog-bound years of depression; this pattern
little resembles that which followed upon our former tariffs, upon those
designed to develop the Country as a whole. Now mills, mines and
factories were being closed; industry after industry was being crippled;
work-orders were going to factories, mines and mills overseas. Tens of
thousands of jobs were being eliminated, to make work abroad for low-
paid labor. Ruin was being brought to scores of fine American communities, and to tens of thousands of American enterprises, large and small.
The agricultural, commercial and industrial map of America was being
made over, and we have been letting it be done.

Not one witness at the hearings on *H.R. 1*—the bill which in 1955
extended to June 1958 the provisions of the Trade Agreements Act—
presented specific, concrete evidence of any nature that American employment had been increased as a result of the theory embodied in the Act.
Cutbacks in employment, however, are supported by clear statistics; they
are real. The policy which has brought Americans into three wars in
less than forty years; which has cost in combat deaths over 600,000 of

our young men; is being pursued without regard to the interests and protection of America's industry, agriculture, worker, investor or family life. It has put millions of our citizens into war production; it has decreased the gainful occupations of normal peacetime work. It has caused unemployment and distress throughout the Land. And the Department of State knows it.

Ever since our forebears' successful Revolution, our people have fought wars to guard their personal liberty, and in the hope that such liberty could be achieved by others. The Thirteen Colonies threw off a system of colonial exploitation which had been imposed upon them pursuant to the acknowledged right of geographical discovery. We are now faced with its modern version. Technology has "brought the world together", and the magnificent manpower and markets developed within these United States have been newly rediscovered. Why should not this discovery carry with it the ancient right of exploitation? Why should not the discoverers again set up the colonial system—or expand their own—and make it this time broader, more lucrative, and modernized? The means of exploitation would be identical with those which held in subjugation our early forebears, and besides, they were in operation elsewhere (though there were, to be sure, signs of acute unrest). The obstacles were not necessarily insuperable, and the vast potential would be worth the effort.

The hypothesis stated, the theory formed, years of education and indoctrination were indicated to make the operation most attractive; perhaps the instruments could even be made alluring to some of the Americans. The instruments are exemplified by GATT.

H.R. 1 was passed. The 1955 extension permits further tariff reductions of 5 percent for each of the following three years, in addition to continuing the overall average of 68 percent reduction already in effect. This tax-paid bonus to foreign producers (and to American producers whose plants are abroad) will add new districts to the 156 distressed areas officially listed by the Department of Labor early in 1955. The areas were located in 32 of the 48 States. Alabama had 7 distressed areas; Arkansas and Connecticut 1 each; Georgia had 2; Illinois, 4; Indiana, 8; Iowa, 2; Kansas, 1; Kentucky, 11; Maine and Maryland, 1 each; Massachusetts, 8; Michigan, 11; Minnesota, 1; Missouri, 4; New Jersey, 2; New Mexico, 1; New York, 8; North Carolina, 5; Ohio, 9; Oklahoma, 2; Oregon, 1; Pennsylvania, 20; Rhode Island and South Carolina, 1 each;

Tennessee, 5; Texas, 1; Vermont, 2; Virginia, 4; Washington, 1; West Virginia, 13; Wisconsin, 4.*

One part of our Country is referred to as Region IV by the Department of Labor. It holds simply tremendous industrial promise if only its industries are permitted to thrive. The area embraces Alabama, Georgia, South Carolina and Tennessee. This should be the most prosperous area in all America if the theory of free trade were right, if it operated according to its claims. Yet, after twenty-two years of the theory in application, there were 15 distressed areas in Region IV. They were: Alexander City, Anniston, Decatur, Florence-Sheffield, Gadsden, Jasper, and Talladega, *Ala.*; Cedartown-Rockmart and Cordele, *Ga.*; Walterboro, *S. Car.*; and Chattanooga, Knoxville, Newport, Johnson City-Kingsport-Bristol, and La Follette-Jellico-Tazewell, *Tenn.* Three of these areas were superdistressed: Jasper, *Ala.*; La Follette-Jellico-Tazewell, and Newport, *Tenn.*

What has caused these communities to suffer, their markets to shrink and in some cases even to dry up? Money? We have more money in circulation than ever in our history. Depression? We have no general depression; we have general (inflated) "prosperity". These are *spot* depressions. They exist, and they are growing. The spot-depression areas exist not in a time of economic adversity but at the height of inflation-prosperity. They are areas affected by a deliberate remaking of the United States' industrial map.

These areas are growing with the pressure of the politico-economic pincers movement.

Not one Senator, not one Member of the House of Representatives, has a voice in the procedure. None of these distressed areas, nor any of those areas which will come, has a single representative to whom its citizens and associations can effectively present their case.

Representative government retains its form. *Power* is in the hands of the executive, alone.

Yet there is a way out of the situation.

The Socialist Republic — the Socialist World State

Do these areas receive gifts, lend-lease, or "aid"? Do they receive handouts such as are sent abroad from the pockets of the working citizens of these United States? Is there within the theory a "Marshall Plan" for

*Further data on such distressed areas may be had from the *Congressional Record* of February 28, 1955 (pp. 1865-83) and of April 1, 1955 (pp. 3607-12).

them? Does the FOA—now become a "specialized agency" of the UN—touch with its Midas wand the people who are affected?

No, not yet. But there is a plan.

The plan is a product of the executive branch. Its essence is a socialist economy for the United States. It proposes that workingmen whose jobs are lost to foreign competition be transferred to other areas; that investors be compensated for their losses, at taxpayers' expense. The State Department suggests that "the government" pay for moving workingmen from one area to another and that owners be paid interest on their losses. When an American industry is destroyed, when unemployment is created, the plan proposes that Congress appropriate the citizens' money to provide unemployment relief for the men displaced. Further appropriations are to underwrite the transportation of displaced workingmen so they can migrate to other areas. The plan, in other words, assumes that the economic map of the United States is to be made over, and outlines steps for its finance. On its human side, in regard to homes and family ties, the plan itself is silent.

The citizens of the Republic, the men and women whose proud heritage derives from the sovereign dignity of the individual, whose Nation was the first in history to by its Constitution set forth clearly the functions of Government and to strictly limit its just powers—are by this reactionary reversion to statism to be set back to the very status from which their forebears successfully rebelled.

The procedure is described as "progress". It is the procedure in force in the U.S.S.R., and it is the procedure in law in Britain.

The United States executive's adaptation of this procedure has influential advocates. In November 1955 the National Planning Association released a 564-page economics study compiled by Dr. D. Humphrey, of Duke University.* The study embraces a broad tariff-slashing program and includes interim relief to American workers and producers who are forced to switch to new industries and localities. Further tariff slashing, the study asserted, would "be one of the most effective means for counteracting the Soviet economic offensive against the free world and for cementing more strongly the unity of the free countries."† The government could provide insurance and grants to local and State agencies to help move workers to areas where employment was available.

Counteraction against the Soviet economic offensive, we find, involves our own adoption of a Soviet economic structure.

---

*Published by the Twentieth Century Fund, New York. 1955.
†United Press release. November 6, 1955.

Extension of the Trade Agreements Act in 1955 was urged by the Secretary of State as an instrument of foreign policy. Therefore, he asserted, if Congress tampered with it the "international repercussions would be major and their consequences would be grave." In other words, the independently cooperative outlook of this Country was beholden to forces possibly foreign to our interests, and certainly beyond our control.

The "emergency" of 1934 had become the "emergency" of 1955. There was a different Secretary of State; the argument had not basically changed. Each "emergency" has brought a further "emergency"; each has called forth exhortations that we proceed with the selfsame policy. Foreign "threat" followed depression; foreign "relief" followed threat. Now relief and threat are commingled, and the politico-economic pincers close in as we permit their ever-increasing pressure upon ourselves.

Workers are to be moved about, exactly as in socialist Russia. Industry, agriculture, shipping, business and trade are to be dependent upon The State—exactly as in socialist Russia. The citizens of this Republic are to be shifted bodily, to homes which somehow, presumably, they will find—exactly as is done in socialist Russia, and precisely as is set forth, more mildly and by law, in socialist Britain.

The pattern is global in its scope.

The political arm of the pincers already has resulted in such pressure that our own laws, made pursuant to our society, framed within the body politic of our own firm Christian traditions, implemented according to our own codes, be "interpreted" "in accordance with the charter and principles of the United Nations". Our men and women, and the civilian component, of our Armed Forces already are made subject to the jurisdiction of scores of other nations—according to "treaty law".

The executive branch of the United States Government, together with the ideological advocates of a global theory, is meanwhile countenancing a gigantic economic mechanism which is designed to bring into being a completely socialist political and economic government of the world.

The program is being followed not by one major political party but by both. Its theory is that peace can be achieved, and that universal prosperity can be brought forth, by abandoning the recently-acquired sovereignty of nationhood and amalgamating all political authorities into one happy and carefree whole. To that theory are being subordinated the normal, natural interests of the citizens of these United States.

Our Nation's Constitution, our Bill of Rights—those historic ten Amendments which set forth the great untappable reservoir of ultimate sovereignty which is reserved to our States and to our people—are being sacrificed, and to a dream-world presumptively governed by "universal law".

Our unique system of individual risk and profit-and-loss, our competitive free economy; our investors, large and small; our producers, workingmen, farmers, shippers; all are to be used as chips in an international poker game in the making of whose rules they have no voice. Yet without them, as the Secretary of State testified before the Senate Finance Committee in 1955, there would be no GATT; there would be no game.

The elected representatives of these, our citizens, have no voice. Only the executive sits in the game. To play with such global chips must be intriguing, and great fun. Only the "house" can win. The "house" is no longer national. It is worldwide.

The engaging possibilities of the situation were not overlooked by traders in Britain. In March of 1942 the Federation of British Industries published its plan. Here is the plan, in part:*

(Par. 11) It is understood that steps are being taken to accumulate certain stocks of essential commodities which would be available for relief purposes . . . . In any case, it is obvious that the primary producer countries will have to help in the supply of food and raw materials; industrial and highly developed countries in the supply of plant, finance and the necessary sea transport.

(Par. 13) . . . . to carry on the task of reconstruction, continuing international cooperation will be needed . . . .

(Par. 14) . . . . we [Britain], above all countries, depend upon world wide trade . . . . [and] we could not collaborate in any international system which was damaging to our own interests . . . .

(Par. 18) . . . . success in reconstruction will depend largely upon the part which America is prepared to play . . . . [and] it is essential that the United Kingdom and the U.S.A. should have an agreed policy . . . .

(Par. 20) In such circumstances the view is widely held in industrial circles in this country that we must, at any rate for some considerable period, rely upon a policy of directive imports . . . . This inevitably implies import and export controls, possibly by quota [or] preferential treatment . . . .

Government by Treason: John Howland Snow. THE LONG HOUSE, INC. New York. 1946 *(pp. 17-20)*.

(Par. 21) [But] contrast this situation with the ideas underlying the policy of the U.S.A. . . . . as defined by members of the U.S.A. Government . . . [where] trade barriers, exchange controls, directive systems of imports and export, discriminatory agreements to facilitate trade between individual countries should be swept away . . . . But for this a highly developed country such as the United Kingdom, is not a matter of economic theory but one of economic life or death . . . .

(Par. 22) . . . . In the past, the basis of American popular opinion has been the protection of American living standards against competition from countries with a lower standard of life and costs.

The executive branch of the American Government has accepted the entire viewpoint set forth above. Prophetic indeed was the British Federation's observation that the protection of American living standards had been our Government's economic outlook—*in the past.*

GATT, the International Finance Corporation, the International Bank and Fund (to which all members of GATT must belong), and other international agencies and authorities, all have been created to advance the plan. And just as the charter of the ITO outlined the purposes for which GATT and the Organization for Trade Cooperation (OTC) were subsequent and entering wedges, so the original British plan outlined the shape of things to come. Like the ITO, the British "Clearing Union" did not itself materialize. But, exactly as the ITO was followed by GATT, the Clearing Union was followed by the International Bank and Fund. And in the House of Lords, John Maynard Keynes described the proposal for the Clearing Union in these words:

> The Clearing Union might become the instrument of policies in addition to those which is its primary purpose to support . . . . The Union might become the pivot of the future economic government of the world.*

Of this potential economic government of the world, the brilliant Garet Garrett immediately wrote: "The ultimate purpose is political, namely, to redistribute the wealth of the world in favor of underprivileged nations."

"From each according to his abilities;" says the Communist Manifesto, "to each according to his needs."

I blame no man who seeks refuge from depression, from deprivation and from war. Countless thousands of our finest citizens have supported this entire theory and its program, convinced in their advocacy by

---

Op. cit., pp. 23, 36.

the persuasive claims which have been authoritatively made in its behalf. Few could know that the program had been long foreseen, that for years it had been creeping into the textbooks of our public schools.

As long ago as 1932, Charles Austin Beard wrote *A Charter for the Social Sciences in the Schools* as a guidebook for teaching in that field. On page 49, Dr. Beard had said:

> By rapidly multiplying ties of trade, capital investment, and intercourse, the United States is being woven ever more closely into a world fabric, drawn into a network of international arrangements.

The lamented Paul W. Shafer, late Member of the House of Representatives from Michigan, and John Howland Snow have documented in their invaluable and basic book, *The Turning of the Tides,* how since the turn of the century the theory has been operating in America's schools. An entire generation of citizens has been subtly influenced by the theory, and indoctrinated toward its acceptance. Many have been persuaded to its advocacy, exactly as were those who accepted at face value the statements issued at the time of the British loan. The official description of that loan read, in part, as follows:

> It will bring prosperity through multilateral trade. It will end economic warfare. The British will abandon their Empire preferences, bilateral agreements, dollar pools, discriminatory import quotas, blocked balances, inconvertible sterling and foreign exchange controls. Trade equilibrium will be restored . . . . *

As you see, these are the exact arguments—at times even word for word—advanced in favor of the Trade Agreements Act, the International Bank and Fund, the GATT, and the Organization for Trade Cooperation (OTC). They are the standard persuasions of the theory.

Men and women within the inner circle of executive government have been carried away by the diagrammed vision of its perfection. (The same is true in civic and cultural organizations throughout our Land.) Others, more intentioned, have guided them, unbeknownst to the ones so led. Well these others knew that the socialist goals of Marx had in front-line practice no proponents more effective than those who embraced the vision, for

> In America, as with other countries affected by Fabian socialism, no overall plan is proposed in forthright fashion for us to accept or reject on its merits. Instead, the planning affects first one segment

---

Op. cit., p. 46.

of our affairs and then another, so that we never do view the process in its total perspective.*

How true this is can be illustrated by those good citizens whose advocacy of free trade appears to have overlooked some of the imperatives of today. However one may accept free trade as an ultimate goal—and I do—a serious question is presently involved, and it is this: Are Fabian socialists quietly promoting free trade behind the scenes? Are others, equally ardent, also behind the program—well aware of why it was advocated by Karl Marx a hundred years ago? He said:

> But, generally speaking, the protective system in these days is conservative, while the free trade system works destructively. It breaks up old nationalities and carries antagonism of proletariat and bourgeoisie to the uttermost point. In a word, the free trade system hastens the social revolution. In this revolutionary sense alone, gentlemen, I am in favor of free trade.†

This combination of communists and Fabian socialists would indeed make clear many things.

The Congress itself—with all the research facilities at its disposal—was persuaded to abdicate its tariff duty and legislative power. And the executive—the well-intentioned, and those who worked with deliberation—took that power and for over two decades have put it unceasingly to work.

Neither the people nor their elected representatives have participated since that time. Their power to participate had been surrendered, to a bland persuasiveness, in 1934.

That is the terrible significance of the political and economic pincers move.

In Time

Industries, shipping men, producers, farmers, growers, working men and women, trade associations, labor organizations, individual citizens, have appeared before the Congress and the executive. They have protested against the impact of the plan. They have appeared singly. Each has been concerned, and naturally so, with his vital individual interests. Each has seen how a single set of circumstances has hit him, and how it hurts.

Not one of these men and women, not one of these associations, has

---

*A. H. Hobbs: *The Vision and the Constant Star.* THE LONG HOUSE, INC. New York. 1956 (*p. 110*).

†Karl Marx, addressing the Democratic Club, Brussels, Belgium; Jan. 9, 1848.

to my knowledge pleaded for more than equal opportunity of access to his own perfectly normal markets. I want to make this clear. These men and women have *not* begged for special dispensation; none has wanted to board a governmental, tax-propelled gravy train.

What each *has* sought is normal, fair and equal opportunity. They do not mind competition. They want an end to the surrender of their domestic market to producers who live abroad. They want a tariff which will equalize the differential between capital and labor costs abroad, and those costs here at home. That is what they want; and that is precisely what they are denied.

A *flexible* tariff system, I believe, would meet with almost universal approval. Such a tariff would assess an import duty equal to the difference between the substantiated invoice value of the imported article and the comparable invoice value of its American-made counterpart. I will not go into the details here, but that is the principle involved.

A flexible tariff system will make it impossible for our economy any longer to be a pawn in an international game of chess. It can actually contribute to a raising of living standards in other lands. If the cost-differential of an article is, say, a dollar, the import duty will be a dollar. The foreign producer, instead of seeing that dollar go into the Treasury of the United States, can increase the rate of profit to his investors, and the rate of wages to his employes. He can use for these purposes one dollar for every unit shipped, and still his product will meet our competitive invoice price. As his costs rise they appear in terms of price, upon his export declaration—and the tariff is automatically lowered. That is the system of a flexible tariff.

It is ultimately possible that every standard commodity in world trade would find its point of landed-cost equality, by this means. The goal of the historical advocates of free trade—which, in truth, is everyone's ideal—could thus in time be reached. It could be reached *practically,* too, and of its own volition; there need be no coercion, no world authority which might work for good or ill.

It might just be possible, too, that by this means the potential higher living standard accruing to human beings overseas would itself contribute in some small, but tangible way to removing one cause for war—to, however minutely, help in a *practical* way the human cause of liberty, and of peace.

Of necessity, I have been brief in regard to the application of a flexible tariff system. Such a system, however, is generally expressive of the views which men and women have voiced at Congressional hearings.

The publicity mill has described their arguments otherwise. Our people have not been given a full and truthful picture.

Citizens and organizations have come to Washington to plead their case. And they have come to Washington with the normal American idea that "the Government" was there, friendly and accessible, ready to hear and weigh their presentations. They have been wrong.

These citizens and their associations erred, and on two major counts. The first is this: They have pleaded with the executive, and the executive is engaged in the application of a theory all its own, one to whose basic premise any economic casualty within America is incidental and expendable. The second error is fundamental, and it is this: Those who have pleaded with elected representatives on Capitol Hill, have been pleading with representatives whose predecessors have abdicated the power of representation, and who themselves have as yet not seen fit to take it back.

Such pleas are a waste of money, of effort, and of time.

There is, however, a procedure which can produce results. A start in this direction has been made; and it is a start—no more. In 1955, the legislative bodies of four States passed resolutions in opposition to extension of the Trade Agreements Act. The States were California, Idaho, Nevada and Utah. The resolutions were right, proper, and in conformity with the due processes of self-government. The four legislatures presented these resolutions to Congress; each of them demanded that the Congress take back its Constitutional power to regulate commerce with foreign nations. Each represented the expressed consensus of informed opinion among the sovereign citizens of those States.*

Precisely here lies our solution.

The solution is not a "law"; it is not mere "opposition"; it is not a "political" matter. I do not believe our interests can be served by extended debates on the merits or the demerits of the program, of GATT, of the OTC, of the Trade Agreements Act, of the Status of Forces Treaty . . . . *unless and until such debates are pointed toward, and result in, dynamic citizen-action.*

The organizations, agencies and authorities which make up the

---

*By mid-1957 the impact of the pincers was being more widely felt. In March, the General Assembly of Pennsylvania memorialized Congress, urging that "existing trade agreements legislation be amended accordingly". Nevada memorialized Congress anew; Alaska petitioned on behalf of its fishing industry; Idaho on behalf of essential minerals; North Dakota on behalf of limitations of petroleum imports to levels recommended by the Cabinet Fuels Committee in February 1955. Florida, Illinois, Maine, Massachusetts, Nebraska, New Hampshire, North Carolina, North Dakota, Oklahoma, South Carolina, Vermont and Wisconsin passed resolutions on one or more phases of the pincers' pressures, coming either from its political jaw, its economic jaw, or both. (See the *Bibliography*, p. 115.)

executive government—whether national or international—are simply not responsive to the people's will. They represent a theory of government which is not ours. It is the ancient, time-worn theory of Power-in-the-State.

It conflicts with every basic tenet of our own new concept, of America's representative self-government.

We have called the old-world concept simply "Big Government", and it must go.

How? Bring back to the City Hall, to the County Court House, to the local school board, to the Legislature and to the Governor of each sovereign State, to the Congress and to the Judiciary, the powers which rightly and properly belong to each—and *only* those powers which rightly and properly belong to each. Once more in its rightful place, the exercise of those powers can be separately controlled—by the voting citizens who choose and elect the personnel.

In the next *national* elections, demand from each and every candidate his answer to this key two-part question:

Will you vote *in favor* of every bill which takes back to your body the power(s) delegated to it by our Constitution; will you vote *against* every bill which adds to (or even continues) power(s) not expressly delegated by the Constitution to another branch of Government?

The answer should be unequivocal—either *Yes* or *No*.

Thirty-two Senatorial seats become vacant each two years. Candidates will come before you for your choice. At the same time, you will be approached by other candidates in your Congressional district, for the entire House of Representatives must come before you every other year. If your candidates will not reply without equivocation to your question, it is your right and duty to get into the nominating caucus and select a man who will. You can have an entirely new Congress within six years. Representative government can be restored in that short time. A *majority* can be had in the Senate in four years; a *majority* can be put into the House of Representatives in twenty-four months. And the House holds the Constitutional power of the purse.

Once more Government will be beholden to the people who elect its personnel.

The majority of the citizens of our Republic may indeed approve the Trade Agreements program, and all of its implications, authorities and costs. The majority, on the other hand, may not approve of it at all.

As the matter now stands, not a single citizen has an effective voice, directly or through the Congress. Ultimate and total power rests with the executive, and nowhere else. The executive may be benign; the executive may be malignant. But there is where power now resides. It is where power resided throughout the ages—until our Colonial forebears took it to themselves, and declared their historic Independence. Then there was put in operation a new theory of government, and for the first time in all history, there was established an effective representative Republic.

Every citizen, every organization, can do his and its part now—to chart the restoration of the representative character of that Republic.

Each can help make government again beholden to the citizens who elect its personnel.

The pincers have not yet fully closed.

Their pressure *can* be removed—and there still is time.

The old theory of Power-in-the-State has again been tried, and it has failed. It is high time we Americans restored our own, the new. In essence, the entire matter is just as simple as this.

The course is clearly marked—by the Declaration of Independence, its compass; and by our matchless Constitution and Bill of Rights, its chart. This is America's Mainline.

APPENDIX

APPENDIX

SOME OPERATIONS OF THE EXECUTIVE

A few details of the pincers' operations will serve to show further how the executive branch is piling plan upon plan and charging the people of the Nation with loss upon loss; always in the interest of "international cooperation", always in the interest of "peace".

I didn't want to put these details in the main text because I thought they might have a tendency to divert you from the theory behind the pincers movement as a whole.

These illustrations can be multiplied by the hundreds, perhaps even by the thousands, so let me stress that they are illustrations *only*. They are not isolated instances, and they have not been selected because of their startling nature or their size, as you will see.

Wheat

If we consumed wheat at the rate our fathers did we would require some 850 million bushels a year. But we are only consuming some 476 million bushels. The changes in our eating habits, particularly among women, has helped bring about this situation. We are now growing about twice as much wheat as we consume. So the taxpayers, including the growers, buy up the surplus. In February of 1956 the Government (the taxpayers) had $2,800,-000,000 tied up in surplus stocks of wheat.

What happens to this accumulation? The Government tries to sell it. How? When? Where? For how much? And where do the proceeds from such sales go?

Take one sale, to France. $6,000,000 worth of surplus wheat was sold to France in the middle of 1956. It was sold at a loss, to be sure, but it was sold. Did the funds from the transaction go into the national treasury as an increment to the people's revenue? No. The wheat was sold for local currency, *i.e.*, for francs. The francs then were left in France, to be made available, by France, to South Viet-Nam. Viet-Nam could use them to purchase industrial commodities. The sale was used to promote French exports to Viet-Nam because Viet-Nam was short of francs.

An agreement was made with Paraguay for the sale of $1,240,000 worth of surplus wheat. Our negotiators accepted in exchange the local currency of Paraguay.

Barter transactions are negotiated by the CCC (Commodity Credit Corporation) whereby wheat is exchanged for strategic and other materials. The CCC's major stocks now include industrial diamonds, ferromanganese, fluorspar and palladium.

In 1956 an agreement was negotiated with West Germany. In exchange for the delivery of coarse grains from America, the ICA (International Co-

97

operation Administration) accepted German marks. These marks were then made available to countries where our "foreign aid" program called for goods available in Germany.

August of 1956 saw the consummation of the largest deal yet made. This agreement was with India. Included in it were 3,500,000 tons of wheat, more than 15 percent of the tonnage then held as surplus. This time the executive branch got $360,000,000 for products which originally had cost America's taxpayers $652,000,000.

The executive again accepted payment in local currency, rupees. From the rupees thus credited, the equivalent of $54,000,000 was transferred as an outright gift to India and some $234,000,000 was loaned to India over a period of forty years. The balance of the $360,000,000 "sales" price was left in India for office expenses in India, and for the purchase of strategic materials *or* for the purchase of Indian goods for other nations.

As an additional gesture to Mr. Nehru, the executive agreed to finance one-half the ocean freight on the products "sold". This one-half came to $54,000,000, which we would pay.

The final day of 1956 saw the executive conclude an agreement with Brazil for the sale of $138,000,000 worth of surplus agricultural products. Included were 1,800,000 metric tons of wheat or wheat flour, billed in this sale at $111,000,000. The payment, again, was in local currency (cruzeiros). A substantial part of the local currency was to be re-loaned to Brazil. The balance was to remain in Brazil and reserved for use in Brazil by agencies of the American executive branch.

Cotton

A two-price situation has been created in regard to cotton. There is a price for the American market, and there is a price for markets abroad. This situation has created an advantage to our foreign competitors of as much as 7c a pound.

Our people are being taxed to subsidize the growing of cotton on the plantations. This results in surplus crops. The surplus is then dumped abroad under the artificial two-price situation and our textile mills are further penalized. The result is another subsidy, paid by the taxpayers. As of the first of August 1956 the Department of Agriculture began paying subsidies on the export of cotton textiles.

The deal with France, the one already referred to under *Wheat*, included the sale of $24,000,000 worth of raw cotton. The same financial conditions were agreed to in regard to cotton as were agreed to with the proceeds from the sale of the wheat.

By August of 1956 the CCC of the Department of Agriculture had disposed of a total of 2,900,000 bales of cotton for export under the 1956-7 disposal program. The average price "received" was between 25c and 26c a pound, compared with the 1956 support price in our own market of 31c a pound. That same August the Secretary of Agriculture announced the largest single agreement for the sale of United States agricultural products yet recorded, the agreement with India. 500,000 bales of cotton were included in this sale, and the $70,000,000 "received" for the cotton were also included in the funds whose distribution has been described under *Wheat*.

By the end of 1956 the executive branch announced it expected to export 6,000,000 bales of cotton by the end of July, 1957, the end of the fiscal year. This would be three times the export during the previous fiscal year, and the highest cotton export for any single year in two decades. Should this estimate prove correct, it will represent the first reduction of Government-held surplus cotton since the fiscal year 1950-1.

We may be sure that this reduction, if it occurs, will be played up for all it is worth. Yet what is the actual situation behind it? What are the facts?

The Trade Agreements Act was passed in 1934. We had been an exporter of cotton, our Nation. It had been a profitable, commercial and private sale. The 1934 Act was supposed to increase that trade; indeed, it was supposed to remove obstacles which were impeding the trade's development.

The Act was passed. The Congress abdicated its Constitutional power. The executive took over.

Plan followed plan. And cost followed cost, all of them reflected in our personal taxes.

The year 1957 presents to us the results of twenty years of executive governance of "foreign trade", and of its increasing regulation of trade within our Land.

We have been obliged to progressively restrict our cotton acreage; our growers are denied the freedom to plant on new cotton lands. They have been compelled to reduce their acreage on lands which they formerly used, and these reductions have caused the unit-cost of production progressively to rise. Our citizens' taxes have steadily been increased to pay to reduce a surplus which has not been reduced, and to prevent new surpluses which have not been prevented. A dramatic expansion of synthetic production has resulted both here and abroad, and the policy has invited the further production of competitive cotton in other parts of the world. No restrictions have been placed on the planting of cotton in countries other than our own. Responsible men have expressed the conviction that our legitimate export trade in cotton will—as the result of the executive policy—be completely wiped out by the end of 1959.

A host of agents have presented to our growers unnumbered quantities of paper forms, and the prohibitions and restrictions of the executive branch have not only reduced the acreage under permissive cultivation, they have enjoined planters from moving on to new lands.

Finally, while one arm of the executive urged vast appropriations of the taxpayers' money for the building of huge dams—to bring new areas under cultivation—another arm of the executive was extolling the idea of a "soil bank"—to take by edict other ("marginal") lands out of production. This program called for a 25 percent cut during 1957 of the acreage under (controlled) cultivation. Should the objective be realized, America's harvested cotton lands would drop to some 13 million acres, the smallest figure in eighty years. Perhaps no cotton acreage is to be "allocated" out of the millions of acres to be watered from the huge federal dams which are being proposed.

I do not know.

Tobacco

What happens when tobacco is purchased under the executive theory and program? What happens after the tobacco is purchased, cured, baled, stored, shipped and insured—all at the taxpayers' expense?

Is there a profit? Does it break even? Do the taxpayers benefit in any way at all?

Here is a single typical illustration.

In the summer of 1956 the executive negotiated an agreement with Britain for the sale of tobacco. The amount involved was $12,000,000. Again the agreement called for payment in local currency, i.e., in pounds. What happened to these pounds? They were appropriated to the defense budget of the United Kingdom and the sterling was earmarked for the building of houses for United States Service personnel who were stationed in Britain.*

Yet the representatives of the British were careful, as always, to guard their own. The purchase of this American tobacco was not to affect the Commonwealth growers, for it was stipulated that the proportion of American tobacco which would be imported would remain strictly limited. This proviso was incorporated in a similar purchase agreement negotiated between the Americans and British the year before.

Groundfish fillets

Here is a relatively small instance, yet it illustrates clearly the theses presented in this book. Groundfish fillets come largely into America from Canada, Iceland and Norway. As imports mounted, men from the industry presented their data to the Tariff Commission. The Commission reported its findings to the executive and recommended a 50 percent increase in duty. What followed is typical.

The President—who must, remember, always rely upon the analyses submitted to him by his executive assistants—rejected in toto the Commission's recommendations. The reasons given for the rejection were these: The recommendations would not solve the difficulties of the domestic industry; the President was reluctant to impose further barriers on trade with friendly

---

*These "counterpart funds"—from the pockets of America's taxpayers—have another, most unexplainable, use. They help reduce the national debts of foreign countries. The following reductions had been accomplished, up to 1957, through counterpart funds alone: *Austria,* $12,500,000; *Denmark,* $130,000,000; *France,* $171,400,000; *Netherlands,* $197,-400,000; *Norway,* $292,700,000; and the *United Kingdom,* $1,706,700,000. In each case, paramountly socialist governments were thus assisted to remain in power.

nations. Further, said the New York *Journal of Commerce* (Dec. 11, 1956), the recent agreement with Iceland permitting the continued stationing of American troops in the country, was considered to have been a factor.

Wool fabrics

In this instance an increase in duty was granted. Britain, France, Japan and Italy, in that order, were our chief suppliers. During 1956 America imported 14,300,000 pounds of wool fabrics, and of this total the United Kingdom supplied two-thirds.

The President was "permitted" to grant an increase in duty; he was enabled to grant it under the permissive provisions of the charter of GATT.

Linen towels

In mid-1956 the President also granted an increase in duty on imports of certain linen towels. The imports affected one section of the industry, and the new duties applied only to towels which were made from flax, hemp and ramie. They did not apply to the greater part of our towel imports.

The 1955 total of the imports affected was only $3,800,000, and the chief suppliers were Japan, Britain and Belgium-Luxembourg. The duty increase had the effect of withdrawing a concession made in Geneva in 1947 with the contracting parties of GATT.

The withdrawal of this concession, however, was soon to be offset. The Department of State early in 1957 launched its program of "compensatory action". It was the sixth such program to follow upon an increase in duty granted to American producers by the executive. This time, eleven entire paragraphs of the Tariff Act of 1930 were included in the Department's list of references, and the enumeration of commodities to be considered for lowered rates filled 2½ pages—all to "compensate" for the concession granted to the makers of linen towels. Further, when a duty is lowered on selected commodities the "compensation" to one country—under the most-favored-nation clause—is extended automatically to all. Each of the affected American industries, industries whose connection with linen towels may be non-existent or remote, thus is obliged to appear before the Tariff Commission *and* the Committee for Reciprocity Information if it would attempt to protect itself from the "compensatory action" of the executive branch of a government whose prime function presumably is to act honorably and primarily in behalf of each and all.

Lighter flints

Representations that this industry was being injured were heard by the Tariff Commission. In December of 1955 the Commission recommended what was in effect a 100 percent increase in duty. It recommended that a 1948 concession under the Trade Agreements Act—by which the duty on flints was lowered by 50 percent—be cancelled.

The recommendations were rejected. In declining to accept them, the

President in November 1956 said, " . . . . it is the firm policy of the United States to seek continuously expanding levels of world trade and investment."

"Buy American" Act

The so-called "Buy American" provisions in government purchase contracts have been subjected to the same kind of pressures and persuasions as have the "Ship American" provisions applying to ocean transport of our taxpayers' "foreign aid". An illustration of executive response to these persuasions is found in an action of the Department of the Interior late in 1955.

In bids submitted for the supply of electrical equipment for federally (taxpayers') financed projects, there was in effect at that time a differential in favor of American bidders. The differential was in some cases as high as 25 percent. In addition to the general differential there was a second differential of 9 percent if a bidding firm were located in an area of "labor surplus". In other words, this second differential was designed to stimulate employment in the "distressed areas" which were listed by the Department of Labor.

The Department of the Interior changed those differentials late in 1955. It issued a new statement of policy. It reduced to 6 percent the (as high as) 25 percent general differential which applied to *all* American bidders, and it reduced to 6 percent the additional differential of 9 percent which applied to "surplus labor" areas.

The result of Interior's new policy statement was immediate. Four contracts, totaling $481,000, were awarded to Italian, British and Swiss manufacturers for the supplying of circuit-breakers for U. S. Government projects.*

Again our taxpayers were to export cash, while they kept good men on "relief" at home.

This action is a clear example of what can happen when power is entrusted to The Total State. You will recall that the principle involved was stated, and developed, in the main body of this text. It was stated explicitly in relation to the policy which is resulting in the transfer of American plants abroad, and in regard to the inducements which are offered to the firms which go. The principle is this: What The Total State may grant, it also may take away.

DUE PROCESS

These illustrations could be continued page after page. Department after executive department increases steadily its tax-borne personnel, in order to keep up with the paper and staff work which are required. Administration

---

*Early in 1957 the Tennessee Valley Authority placed orders for two of the largest transformers ever built, for installation at the TVA's new power plant at Gallatin, Tenn. The orders went abroad, to the English Electric Company of Stafford. The same issue of *British Affairs* which carries this story also announces the following: "The British firm, Thomas De La Rue, has received orders from the U. S. Treasury for new high speed banknote printing machinery worth $1½ million."

after administration promises—before election—to cut down. Yet the Department of State alone increased its appropriation in 1956 by $24,000,000, and its personnel rose by 2519 employes over the 20,748 persons it had on its payroll a year before. (This figure does not take into account, for instance, the 6395 employes of the FOA who were transferred to State during that year.) The headquarters of this Department now require a new $54,000,000 building, for which the appropriation has been authorized.

By the summer of 1957 civilian employment in the executive branch totalled 2,394,099—an increase of 30,000 employes over the previous fiscal year. Annual salaries rose by over $500,000,000, to more than eleven billion dollars. Nor does this figure include the salaries—approaching a quarter billion dollars annually—paid to foreign nationals not on the regular payroll. These huge totals are for the *executive branch alone.*

As a corollary to this ominous growth of power and of all that commonly goes with power, the executive branch constantly, steadily and unceasingly reminds our citizens that any review, or change, in any international agreement which it may propose, will "seriously impair" our foreign relations; in fact, "peace itself may hang in the balance". Due process of American law, required by the mandates of the Constitution, is studiously ignored. To be sure, provisional words and phrases are in the agreements themselves; they are frequently quite clearly written. Yet they are no more than words, and every act and gesture of the executive vis-à-vis the people shows it.

This contrasts curiously with the situation overseas. It has taken nearly ten years to persuade the Swiss that a way might be found by which they would feel free to become members of GATT.

Articles XI and XV of GATT contravene the Swiss constitution. And it was unrealistic, said the Swiss, to suppose that their people would approve amendments to their constitution in order to satisfy the provisions of GATT, or that they would agree to eliminate laws which they had passed for the protection of their own agriculture. It is now expected that Switzerland will be enabled to become a member of GATT by the end of 1957 or the first half of 1958. This will be hailed as a great forward step in the program of "international cooperation".

No one has heard, and no one will hear, that the proud Swiss people stood in the way of "international cooperation" for ten long years and then, and only then, entered into negotiations upon the sound premise that they were going to be adequately protected in the process.

Festivities in "International Cooperation"

The government of Viet-Nam is, I am sure, one of "the democracies". It doubtless also is one of the units which comprise "the free world". It has the problem of inflation, too. It is combating that problem with measures which, strangely enough, are almost as common in "fighting socialism" as they are common to socialist Britain and to the socialist Soviet.

Viet-Nam has a Secretary for National Economy. On August 10, 1956 the Secretary issued an order. The order set forth the precise profit margins to be permitted on imported cotton and silk fabrics, at wholesale and at retail levels. For every shipment, importers were to report to the Price Control Administration the quantity of silk and cotton fabrics received, the license number, the date and the amounts of foreign exchange allotted, the country of origin of the fabrics, the deadline for receiving the balance of a partial shipment, the f.o.b. and c.i.f. cost of the goods, the wholesale and retail prices of each commodity, the names and addresses of customers, the quantity and description of the goods, and the wholesale and retail prices of each article for all sales involving more than 500 meters of fabric. The transport outside the Saigon-Cholon and Giadinh city limits of more than 500 meters of cotton and silk fabrics was permissible only by authorization of the Price Control Administration.

Eight days later an order was issued limiting the amount of petroleum stocks which individuals and shopkeepers might hold, and requiring authorization for the transport of amounts in excess of 38 liters.

But, inflation or no inflation, there was in the offing a celebration which in Viet-Nam is know as *Tet*. For this celebration many goods were in short supply. Something must be done. Someone must produce a plan. The Secretary for National Economy produced the plan.

He prepared a schedule of imports. The schedule covered the third quarter of 1956, and called for a substantial rise in the quantity of goods brought in. The increased imports would provide for *Tet*. The amount totalled $76,500,000.

There remained the matter of how to finance these imports, and this matter was happily resolved.

The $76,500,000 was produced out of America's "foreign aid".

Now smile, for you taxpayers all helped make these good people happy.

Tet, in Viet-Nam, is the name for the annual New Year's festivities.

CLASSIFIED BIBLIOGRAPHY

The references are grouped under six general headings and, under each heading, as nearly as possible listed by subject and in order of time. Many of the documents contain material which is pertinent to more than one subject, while the *Hearings* sometimes contain in a single volume material which is directly pertinent to the entire presentation.

Several abbreviations are employed: The *Federal Register* appears simply as *FR*; a Library of Congress Catalog Number as *LC*; and the number and session of a Congress are signified by numbers, as for example, 84/1.

The classification should facilitate confirmation of the theses presented, as well as the access to material of special concern to any citizen, association or corporation.

We hope the *Classified Bibliography* will render such a service.

THE PUBLISHERS

Official Documents and Publications
(a) Documents of the House and Senate

Hearings on the original Trade Agreements Act. *House Report 1000* and *Senate Report 871*. 73/2. 1934

THE TRADE AGREEMENTS ACT OF 1934. *Public Law 316*, 73d Congress. Approved June 12. (The entire Act contains less than 1200 words.) Also *Statutes at Large*, Vol. 48; p. 943

——, 1949 extension of. *Hearings*, House Committee on Ways and Means. 81/1. Feb. 1949. 776 pp. *LC*:HF 1731 .A5 1949

——. *Hearings*, Senate Finance Committee. 81/1. Feb. 1949. 867 pp. *LC*:HF 1731 .A514 Pt. I

——, 1951 extension of. *Hearings*, House Committee on Ways and Means. 82/1. Jan. 1951. 624 pp

——, 1955 extension of. Text of *H.R. 1. Calendar No. 242*, 84/1. Feb. 21, 1955

——. *Hearings*, House Committee on Ways and Means. *House Report 50*. 84/1. Feb. 14, 1955

——. *Hearings*, Senate Finance Committee. 84/1. PART 1; 626 pp. PART 2; 1267 pp. PART 3; 1909 pp. March 1955

——. REPORT AND MINORITY VIEWS. *Senate Report 232*. 84/1. Apr. 28, 1955

——. Act extended to June 30, 1958. *Public Law 86*, 84/1. Approved June 21, 1955

S. 1723. 84/1. Introduced by Senator Malone on Apr. 18, 1955

STRATEGIC MATERIALS. *Hearings*, Special Subcommittee on Minerals, Materials and Fuels Economics, Senate Committee on Interior and Insular Affairs. PART 1: DEPARTMENT OF THE INTERIOR, BUREAU OF MINES. Oct. 1953. 351 pp

PART 2: STOCKPILE. Includes testimony of Defense Department and of tactical military experts. Also includes Harry Dexter White's correspondence, with his letter of 1/10/45 wherein he suggested a $10,000,000,000 credit to the Soviet and that the U. S. had become a "have-not" nation (p. 658). Sept. 1953-Feb. 1954. 825 pp

PART 3: TITANIUM. Sept. 1953-Apr. 1954. 791 pp

PART 4: INTERNATIONAL MATERIALS CONFERENCE. Contains (pp. 194-7) White's proposed credit of $5,000,000,000 to the Soviet and that we be supplied with critical materials by the Soviet. The index, under *White*, carries further data. Oct. 1953-Jan. 1954. 1181 pp

PART 5: COMMODITY TRADE AGREEMENTS UNDER UNITED NATIONS AUSPICES. Reproduces UN and UNESCO publications concerning trade, "underdeveloped countries", and allied subjects. May 26, 1954. 447 pp

PART 6: PETROLEUM, GAS AND COAL. Nov. 1953-Feb. 1954. 1340 pp

PART 7: TARIFFS AND TAXES AND THEIR RELATIONSHIP TO CRITICAL MATERIALS. Oct. 1953-Mar. 1954. 320 pp

PART 8: STAFF STUDY OF THE PALEY COMMISSION REPORT. Apr. 9, 1954. 783 pp

PART 9: URANIUM, COLUMBIUM, COBALT, RUTILE; AND MISCELLANEOUS STRATEGIC RAW MATERIALS OF AGRICULTURAL ORIGIN. Nov. 1953-Mar. 1955. 490 pp

PART 10: INDUSTRIAL REPRESENTATIVES OF PRODUCERS AND USERS OF STRATEGIC AND CRITICAL MATERIALS. Sept. 1953-May 1954. 852 pp

PART 11: SYNTHESIS, SUBSTITUTIONS AND REPLACEMENTS OF SCARCE STRATEGIC MATERIALS. Sept.-Nov. 1954. 494 pp

PART 12: TITANIUM. (Supplement to PART 3) Oct.-Dec. 1954. 169 pp. PARTS 1-12 inclusive: *LC:HC 106 5 .A5 1954g*

——— ACCESSIBILITY OF STRATEGIC AND CRITICAL MATERIALS TO THE UNITED STATES IN TIME OF WAR AND FOR OUR EXPANDING ECONOMY. *Senate Report 1627*, 83/2. July 9, 1954. 415 pp

——— CRITICAL MATERIALS. FACTORS AFFECTING SELF-SUFFICIENCY WITHIN NATIONS OF THE WESTERN HEMISPHERE. *Senate Doc. 83*, 84/1. (Supplement to *Senate Report 1627*) July 28, 1955. 619 pp

THE OTC. President's message requesting enactment of enabling legislation; Articles of Agreement of the proposed OTC. *House Doc. 140*, 84/1. Apr. 14, 1955

———, *Hearings*. House Committee on Ways and Means. 84/2. Mar. 1956. 1444 pp

———, AND GATT. THE AGREEMENT ON THE ORGANIZATION OF TRADE COOPERATION. *House Report 2007*, 84/1. Apr. 18, 1956

KARL MARX ON FREE TRADE. Address of Hon. George W. Malone to the Senate, Feb. 27, 1951. Marx' quotation is on p. 4 of the reprint made by the Senator's office.

STATE DEPARTMENT PERSONNEL. Hon. A. E. Johansen, *Mich. Press Release*. May 2, 1956

"DISTRESSED AREAS." *S. 2892, AREA ASSISTANCE ACT OF 1956*, and *S. 2663*, the *AREA REDEVELOPMENT ACT*. 84/1. *S. 964*, the *AREA REDEVELOPMENT ACT OF 1957*. 85/1. (Copies available from any member of the Senate)
TRADE ADJUSTMENT ACT OF 1957. *S. 2907*, 85/1, introduced by Senator Kennedy, *Mass*. (See also, *Congressional Record*, Aug. 30, 1957; pp. 15091-2)

INVESTIGATION OF THE FINANCIAL CONDITION OF THE UNITED STATES. *Hearings*, Senate Finance Committee, 85/1, Part 3. Aug. 1957; 392 pp. Discussions between the Chairman of the Board of Governors, Federal Reserve System, and members of the Committee. Sen. Malone's exchanges with the witness (169 pp) are most informative.

(b) Documents of the Executive Branch
MINES AND MINING. War Production Board Order *L-208. FR:* Vol. 8, p. 12007. 1942

Bulletin 2411. Department of State. Nov. 1945

THE ITO. *The Geneva Charter of an International Trade Organization.* "At its first meeting in February 1946, the [UNESCO] Council adopted a resolution calling for an international conference on trade and employment and to consider the creation of an international trade organization . . . . and prepare a detailed draft charter for such an organization." First session, Oct. 1946. Dept. of State Pub. 2950, Commercial Policy Series 107. 1947. *LC:* HF 1455 .A3
────── *Havana Charter for an International Trade Organization.* UN Conference on Trade and Employment. Dept. of State Pub. 3117, C.P. Series 113. Apr. 1947 (Also No. 3206, C.P. Series 114; Mar. 24, 1948)
────── *Charter for the International Trade Organization of the United Nations* (Preliminary Draft). Articles of the ITO charter as drafted by the London conference, Oct.-Nov. 1946. D. of S. Pub. 2728, C.P. Series 98. 1947. 68 pp
────── *American Trade Policy.* D. of S. Pub. 3091; C.P. Series 110. Jan. 18, 1948

GATT. *A Constitution for World Trade.* D. of S. Pub. 2964; C.P. Series 108. Nov. 1947
────── *Analysis of General Agreement on Tariffs and Trade.* D. of S. Pub. 2983; C.P. Series 109. Nov. 1947
────── Executive Order of Dec. 16, 1947. *FR*, Vol. 12, p. 8867. Proclamation 2761A
────── GENERAL AGREEMENT ON TARIFFS AND TRADE. D. of S. Pub. 3107; C.P. Series 111. Apr. 1948, Vol. 1. (VOLS. 2, 3 and 4, *Schedules of Tariff Concessions*, may be obtained from the International Documents Service, Columbia University Press, 2960 Broadway, New York 27, at $1.50 per volume. *Schedule XX, Most-Favored Nation Tariff*, is available from the Government Printing Office, Washington, D. C., at 50c a copy.)
Except for the Executive Order of Dec. 1947, the last eight items' *LC* reference is HF 1455 .A3

Postwar Foreign Policy Preparation, 1939-1945. The program was generally approved by the President in December 1941. The Committee references herein are taken from pp. 219, 222, 224 and 353. The committee members who are named are taken from pp. 3, 63-5, 73-4 and 78.

STATUS OF FORCES AGREEMENT. Certified copy of the agreement; the President's letter of transmittal (6/16/52); Resolution of Ratification, with Reservations, as agreed to by the Senate on July 15, 1953. Senate, *Executive T.* 82/2
———— AN AGREEMENT RELATING TO THE STATUS OF THE NORTH ATLANTIC TREATY ORGANIZATION. Proposals regarding U.S.-NATO relations, together with corrections of certain errors in the original French text. Senate, *Executive U.* 82/2. June 16, 1952
———— STATUS OF INTERNATIONAL MILITARY HEADQUARTERS SET UP PURSUANT TO THE NORTH ATLANTIC TREATY. Senate, *Executive B.* 83/1. Feb. 27, 1953. (Signed at Paris Aug. 28, 1953)
———— AGREEMENTS RELATING TO THE STATUS OF THE NORTH ATLANTIC TREATY ORGANIZATION, ARMED FORCES, AND MILITARY HEADQUARTERS. Senate, *Executive Report No. 1.* Apr. 28, 1953

THE PALEY REPORT. *Resources for Freedom.* Report of the President's Materials Policy Commission. 5 volumes in one binding. *LC: House Docs. Vol. 20, 82/2, 1952.* (11616, No. 1)

SURPLUS AGRICULTURAL PRODUCTS. Agreements with Viet-Nam and Paraguay. Dept. of Agriculture *Press Release.* May 4, 1956
———— France-Viet-Nam agreement. Dept. of State *Bulletin.* May 7, 1956
———— *World Tobacco Analysis,* International Trade Issue. Dept. of Agriculture, May 1956
———— *Foreign Agriculture Circular,* FT9-56. Breakdown of tobacco sales to other countries under Title 1 of Public Law 480, for the period ending June 30, 1956. Dept. of Agriculture, Foreign Agricultural Service. Aug. 24, 1956
———— *CCC; Report of Financial Condition and Operations as of June 30, 1956.* Operations of the Commodity Credit Corporation, including barter transactions. D. of A. June 30, 1956
———— *The Cotton Situation.* Cotton exports, 1956-7. D. of A. July 27, 1956
———— *Cotton Production.* Crop estimates for 1956. D. of A. Aug. 8, 1956
———— Agreement with India. D. of A. *Press Release.* Aug. 29, 1956
———— *Increasing U. S. Farm Exports.* D. of A., For. Agri. Serv. Nov. 1956
———— *The World Agricultural Situation, 1957.* D. of A., For. Agri. Serv. Dec. 1956
———— Agreement with Brazil. D. of A. *Press Release,* Dec. 31, 1956; Dept. of State *Press Release,* Dec. 31, 1956; *The Journal of Commerce,* New York, Jan. 2, 1957
———— *The Fifth Semi-Annual Report on Activities Carried on Under Public Law 480.* Figures on disposal of surplus agricultural products, July-Dec. 1956. (Barter contracts since July 1954 total $745,000,000.) Transmitted to Congress by the President on Jan. 14, 1957
———— *Competitive Position of United States Farm Products Abroad, 1957.* D. of A., For. Agri. Serv. Jan. 1957

—— *Foreign Agricultural Trade of the United States*. By countries, fiscal year 1955-6. D. of A., For. Agri. Serv. Jan. 1957
—— *Foreign Crops and Markets*. D. of A., For. Agri. Serv. Jan. 29, 1957
—— *Idem*. Feb. 4, 1957

"DISTRESSED AREAS." *Labor Market Developments in Major Areas*. (Bimonthly.) Dept. of Labor, Bureau of Employment Security. May 1955. (By Press Release *USDL 1150*, the classification system was altered. Comparison of figures later than those given in this book should be made with this change in mind.)

(c) *References in the* Congressional Record—*floor debates and Appendix*
General
SUMMARY OF DEBATES DURING 1947, AND EXCERPTS FROM 1948, ON THE OVERALL PROGRAM. Compiled and bound by Senator Malone's office. (Not printed at Government expense) 200 pp
—— *Idem*. SUMMARY OF 1949 DEBATES. (These two volumes have been used with much success by school debating teams)

TABLES OF IMPORT DUTIES, by year, from 1791 through 1952, and partial for 1953 and 1954. Jan. 12, 1955; pp. 360-2

A CONSPIRACY TO DESTROY AMERICAN WORKINGMEN AND SMALL INVESTORS: Hon. George W. Malone. Feb. 28, 1955; pp. 1865-82

THE DOMESTIC ECONOMY VS. FOREIGN RELATIONS: Hon. George W. Malone. Includes tables of "distressed areas", by reason and by location. Apr. 1, 1955; pp. 3607-12

Trade Controls by Other Countries. Tabulated by country and controls. May 4, 1955; pp. 4737-9
—— IMPORT CONTROLS ON AMERICAN PRODUCTS; ALL NATIONS. Aug. 13, 1957; 13292-4

TRADE AND/OR PAYMENTS AGREEMENTS BETWEEN THE SINO-SOVIET BLOC AND OTHER COUNTRIES. Aug. 13, 1957; 13297
—— BETWEEN OTHER NATIONS AND THE SOVIET BLOC. *Idem*; 13303

ANNUAL PER CAPITA INCOME IN 20 MAJOR TRADING NATIONS (table). Aug. 15, 1957; A6701

TARIFFS OR SOCIALISM. Address by Edgar M. Queeny, chairman of the board, Monsanto Chemical Co. The address covers tariffs, the ITO, GATT, OTC; wheat, cotton goods and chemicals; the UN charter, Genocide Convention, Covenant on Human Rights; and Fabian Socialism and world government. Jan. 20, 1956; pp. A598-602

FOREIGN AID FOREVER?: Hon. A. E. Johansen, *Mich*. June 21, 1956; pp. 9717-8

CRITICAL MATERIALS, WESTERN HEMISPHERE DEFENSE, etc.: Hon. George W. Malone. Apr. 17, 1957; pp. 5277-92 and Apr. 18, 1957; p. 5366 *e.s.*

FOREIGN TRADE AND THE NATIONAL ECONOMY: Hon. George W. Malone. May 15, 1957; pp. 6234-40

CONSTITUTIONAL INTEGRITY AND FOREIGN TRADE: Hon. Philip J. Philbin, *Mass.* June 5, 1957; pp. A4372-3

THE THEORY AND PRACTICE OF FREE TRADE: Hon. Thomas J. Lane, *Mass.* June 13, 1957; 8104

TRADE AGREEMENTS IN EFFECT UNDER THE 'ACT OF 1934, AS AMENDED. Aug. 13, 1957; 13296

"DISTRESSED AREAS." Dept. of Labor listing for July 1957. Aug. 30, 1957; 15108

COUNTERPART FUNDS. Used to pay foreign countries' national debts. One item of a 9-part study made by the Legislative Reference Service of the Library of Congress at the request of Hon. Ralph W. Gwinn, *N. Y.*, and 16 other Members, of both Parties. The study is titled *The Adverse Effects of Expanding Government.* Published in condensed form by *Nation's Business* (Sept. 1957). Aug. 29, 1957; A7245

Agriculture

General	FACTS FOR FARMERS AND OTHER AMERICANS: Hon. John Marshall Butler, *Md.* Jan. 30, 1956; pp. A883-4
Cotton	TESTIMONY OF COTTON INDUSTRY BEFORE COMMITTEE ON AGRICULTURE: Hon. Hale Boggs, *La.* June 5, 1956; pp. A4458-68
Tobacco	ACREAGE CUTS: 5% in 1955; 12% in 1956; 20% in 1957—37% in three years. Mar. 20, 1957; p. A2258
Butterfat	BUTTERFAT IMPORTS: Hon. Edward J. Thye, *Minn.* Imports threaten increase of taxpayers' burden by further CCC losses. July 12, 1957; 10334-5
Wool	THE PROBLEMS OF THE SHEEP INDUSTRY: Hon. Frank A. Barrett, *Wyo.*, and others. Sheep population drops from 49 to 26 million head; how the Trade Agreements program affects the industry. Aug. 28, 1957; 14687 *e.s.*
Surplus Disposal	AGRICULTURAL COMMODITIES: DISPOSAL UNDER *PL 480.* Tables, by countries and by disposal of funds. Apr. 1, 1957; pp. 4329-31
Soil Bank	WE ALREADY HAVE AN IMMENSE SOIL BANK: Hon. Craig Hosmer, *Cal.* Jan. 12, 1956; pp. 405-6

Industry

Plywood	IMPORTATION OF FOREIGN PLYWOOD: Hon. H. Strom Thurmond, *S. Car.* Feb. 18, 1957; pp. 1887-9
———	RESTRICTIONS ON THE IMPORTATION OF HARDWOOD PLYWOOD: Hon. H. Strom Thurmond, *S. Car.*, and other Senators. Mar. 14, 1957; pp. 3227 and 3260-3
———	IMPORTS OF FOREIGN PLYWOOD ARE ROBBING THOUSANDS OF AMERICAN WORKERS OF THEIR JOBS: Hon. Russell V. Mack, *Wash.* Aug. 29, 1957; A7276-7
Linen Towels	What happened after the duty was reduced in 1956. Mar. 21, 1957; p. 3696
———	To "compensate" for duty reduction, products classified under 11 tariff paragraphs are listed for lowered rates. June 5, 1957; pp. A4367-8

Textiles   THE THREAT TO THE TEXTILE INDUSTRY AND TO COTTON GROWERS
                  IN THE UNITED STATES: Hon. John J. Riley, *S. Car.* June 5, 1956;
                  pp. A4472-3
————   SHAPING THE TEXTILE FUTURE. Address by F. E. Grier of
                  Greenwood, S. Car., presiding at the eighth annual meeting of
                  the American Cotton Manufacturers Institute at Palm Beach,
                  Fla., Apr. 4, 1957. May 8, 1957; pp. A3507-8
————   Over 100,000 people out of jobs in last ten years. Hon. Philip J.
                  Philbin, *Mass.* June 4, 1957; pp. 7430-1
————   Seven more mills close, from Maine to the Carolinas, adding
                  further to the "Distressed Areas" and unemployment. One of
                  these mills had been operating for more than a hundred years.
                  Sept. 11, 1957; A7409-11
Woolens,   WOOLEN AND WORSTED IMPORTS. Statement of Wool Manufac-
Worsteds   turers' Council of the Northern Textile Assn., Boston, Mass.
                  May 8, 1957; pp. A3495-6. (Includes figures on imports)
————   146 woolen industries liquidated within the last decade. Hon.
                  Edith Nourse Rogers, *Mass.* June 3, 1957; pp. 7355 and A4254-5
POTTERY,   OPEN LETTER TO PRESIDENT EISENHOWER: WILL YOU LET OUR
CERAMICS   INDUSTRY DIE? May 27, 1957; pp. A4093-4
————   Letter to Hon. Wayne L. Hays, *Ohio,* from a pottery executive.
                  May 28, 1957; pp. A4130-1
————   NEED FOR A PROTECTIVE TARIFF LAW: Hon. John E. Henderson,
                  Ohio. Discussion of GATT and the OTC, with tables of house-
                  hold pottery and ceramic wall and floor tile imports, by country
                  of origin, from 1947 to June 1957. Sept. 19, 1957; A7704-6
Watches   THE DOMESTIC WATCH INDUSTRY: Hon. Carl T. Curtis, *Nebr.*
                  Tariff Commission's figures on jeweled- and pin-lever move-
                  ment imports. At 13,500,000 units, imports up 30% in 1956
                  over 1955. Aug. 8, 1957; 12707
————   IMPORTATION OF SWISS WATCHES: Hon. Everett M. Dirksen, *Ill.*
                  The industry presents a critical situation. Aug. 29, 1957; A7229-
                  30
Air   AIRLINES, DOMESTIC AIRLANES: KLM—ROYAL DUTCH AIRLINES
Transport   ROUTES: Hon. Styles Bridges, *N. H.* State Dept. negotiates with
                  the Netherlands to extend KLM's services to domestic American
                  airports; favors foreign (80% state-owned) lines over (privately-
                  owned) American lines. Parallel of these negotiations with the
                  policy affecting the American merchant marine. Mar. 29, 1957;
                  pp. 4260-1
————   BILATERAL AIR TRANSPORT AGREEMENTS: Hon. Homer Capehart,
                  Ind. May 28, 1957; p. 7022
————   SAVE OUR AMERICAN AVIATION INDUSTRY: Hon John Jarman,
                  Okla. Threat of proposed use, by foreign carriers, of our do-
                  mestic airlanes. July 11, 1957; 10295-6
Fishing   UNITED STATES FISHERIES: Hon. Robert G. Wilson, *Cal.* Jan. 12,
Industry   1956; pp. 406-7

——— PROBLEMS OF THE TUNA FISHING INDUSTRY: Hon. Warren E. Magnuson, *Wash.* June 21, 1957; A4954-5

——— THE TUNA CRISIS: Hon. Warren E. Magnuson, *Wash.* Import figures of albacore tuna, canned in Japan, and our own West Coast catch from 1950-5. July 17, 1957; 10803-5

——— NEED FOR EXPANDING TRADE. Letter and Statement of the American Tugboat Ass'n., San Diego, Cal. Recommendations for alleviation. Aug. 2, 1957; A-6286-8,

——— TUNA IMPORT REGULATION: Hon. Cecil R. King, *Cal.* Detailed outline of the industry's distress, together with legislation introduced for amelioration. Aug. 13, 1957; A6608-10

Shipping EFFORTS TO ELIMINATE THE PROVISIONS THAT 50% OF GOVERNMENT-GENERATED CARGOES BE CARRIED IN AMERICAN FLAGSHIPS: Hon. John Marshall Butler, *Md.* June 4, 1956; pp. A4390-1

——— CARGO PREFERENCE LEGISLATION: Hon. John Marshall Butler, *Md.* June 4, 1956; pp. A4390-1

——— 50-50 LAW HOLDS OCEAN FREIGHT RATES DOWN AND EXPEDITES AGRICULTURE SURPLUS DISPOSAL PROGRAM: Hon. Thor C. Tollefson, *Wash.* How foreign cargo rates rise when American Flagships are not available. Mar. 14, 1957; p. A2082

Residual RESIDUAL OIL, AND OTHER IMPORTS: Hon. James E. Van Zandt,
Oil *Pa.* Impact of the program on a number of industries, including coal. Apr. 10, 1957; p. A2871

——— FOREIGN OIL IMPORTS: Hon. Joseph C. O'Mahoney, *Wyo.* Includes telegram to the President, signed by 32 Governors, urging protective action. July 17, 1957; 1085

Rubber THE AMERICAN TAXPAYER AND BRITISH RUBBER PRODUCTION: Hon. H. R. Gross, *Iowa.* The British announce they will build, in the Soviet, the largest tire factory in the world outside the U. S. An article by C. Wilson Harder, president of the Nat'l. Fed. of Independent Business, is included. July 22, 1957; A-5883-4

Mining Domestic Zinc Industry. Situation in Oklahoma. Apr. 30, 1957; pp. 5511-6

——— ACCESSIBILITY OF CRITICAL MATERIALS—HIGHER TEMPERATURE ALLOYS: Hon. George W. Malone. May 20, 1957; pp. 6435-42

——— DOMESTIC MINING INDUSTRY: Hon. Henry Aldous Dixon, *Utah.* Mines closing; a new policy needed. June 14, 1957; 8145-7

——— THE IMPORTANCE OF TUNGSTEN: Hon. Mike Mansfield, *Mont. Idem*; 8165-6

——— END OF THE ROAD FOR ANOTHER LEAD-ZINC MINE: Hon. William A. Dawson, *Utah.* June 17, 1957; A4789

——— PUBLIC LAW 733—THE MINERALS PURCHASE ACT (84th Congress): Hon. George W. Malone, *Nev.* Includes FOREIGN EFFORT TO BREAK TUNGSTEN MARKET. June 24, 1957; 9054-9

——— RELIEF FOR THE DOMESTIC LEAD-ZINC INDUSTRY AND WORKERS: Hon. Arthur V. Watkins, *Utah.* Another mine closes, this one in New Jersey. Detailed statement of the industry's position, and tables of world prices and production, made on July 22 before the Senate Finance Committee by Charles E. Schwab, chairman of the Emergency Lead-Zinc Committee. July 25, 1957; 11476-80

—— THE LEAD-ZINC CRISIS. Statement of Miles P. Romney, Mgr., Utah Mining Assn. Aug. 13, 1957; A6597-8

—— THE FUTURE OF THE LEAD AND ZINC INDUSTRY: Hon. Charles H. Brown, *Mo.* The developing situation, together with remarks by other Members. Aug. 22, 1957; 14293-9

—— THE DOMESTIC MINING INDUSTRY: Hon. Alan Bible, *Nev.* Its situation; legislation imperative at next Session. Aug. 30, 1957; 15166-8

GATT THE PATTERN OF GATT: Hon. Cleveland M. Bailey, *W. Va.* Jan. 30, 1956; pp. 1381-4

—— GATT AND LABOR: Hon. Cleveland M. Bailey, *W. Va.* Labor unions which are opposed to GATT. June 4, 1956; p. A4402

—— Indefinite freeze proposed on U. S. right to withdraw tariff concessions under GATT: Hon. Thor C. Tollefson, *Wash.* June 18, 1957; 8584

—— REGULATION OF FOREIGN COMMERCE AND TARIFF RATES: Hon. Henderson L. Lanham, *Ga.* How State Dept. flouts Congress under GATT, etc.; how GATT embraces "the seed of possibly reshaping the world economy . . . " June 24, 1957; 9142-3. (Material noted as missing in this reference will be found in the issue of June 26; pp. 9352-3)

OTC CONSTITUTIONALITY OF OTC: Hon. Carl T. Durham, *N. Car.* June 11, 1956; pp. A4629-34

—— ORGANIZATION FOR TRADE COOPERATION: Hon. Richard M. Simpson, *Pa.* June 27, 1956; pp. A5087-8

—— OTC. SUPPLEMENTAL VIEWS ON H.R. 5550: Hon. Thomas B. Curtis, *Mo.* July 11, 1956; pp. A5434-8

—— President's Message urging U. S. membership in. "America's foreign trade has grown rapidly under our reciprocal trade agreements policy." Apr. 3, 1957; p. 4464

—— OTC: Hon. Cleveland M. Bailey, *W. Va.* Membership in the OTC would make elections feckless, and no Member of Congress could any longer represent his constituents. "The State Department would be satisfied". Apr. 8, 1957; pp. 4736-7

—— OTC AND THE UNITED NATIONS: Hon. Henderson L. Lanham, *Ga.* Text of UN Resolution in regard to trade (*GA/1450*, Feb. 20, 1957), and how the OTC can make its own rules. May 9, 1957; pp. A3530-1

Foreign Aid AMERICAN TAXPAYERS CONTRIBUTE STAGGERING SUM FOR FOREIGN AID: Hon. Lawrence H. Smith, *Wisc.* TABLE I: Foreign grants, by program; TABLE II: by country and program; TABLE III: foreign credits utilized, by program. (All tables inclusive from July 1, 1945 through June 30, 1956) Apr. 1, 1957; pp. A2595-2602

—— FOREIGN AID REVERSE GRANTS AND REPAYMENTS BY FOREIGN COUNTRIES, SECTION 2: Hon. Lawrence H. Smith, *Wisc.* TABLE I: Net grant aid, war period, July 1, 1940-June 30, 1956; TABLE II: reverse grants and returns on grants, by country and program, postwar period, July 1, 1945-June 30, 1956; TABLE III: repayments of loans and other credits, by country, war and postwar period, July 1, 1940-June 30, 1956. Apr. 18, 1957; pp. A3106-8

—— FOREIGN AID: Hon. Otto E. Passman, *La.* Over 2,000 programs going on, in 66 of the 85 countries of the world. Unexpended balance of 8¼ billion dollars remained on Jan. 31, 1957 when new requests for 4.4 billion dollars were made. Apr. 17, 1957; pp. 5303-6

—— IRRIGATION, POWER, AND FLOOD-CONTROL PROJECTS UNDER ICA: Hon. A. L. Miller, *Nebr.* Tables of projects, their costs and obligations. May 7, 1957; pp. A3426-8

—— WHO GOT IT?: Hon. Alvin E. O'Konski, *Wisc.* Foreign aid, by country and amount, since June 30, 1945. June 21, 1957; A4970

—— Text of Minority Report, House Committee on Foreign Affairs (1957) on the Mutual Security program. As of June 30, 1957 an estimated $6,232,734,000 remained in the pipeline of undelivered materials, services and commodities. Some $1,114,900,000 were further available in foreign currencies, these being unexpended receipts under the agricultural disposal program. A table lists the funds "received" from the beginning of the program, by country and by planned use, to Feb. 28, 1957. Inserted by Hon. Marguerite Stitt Church, *Ill.* July 16, 1957; 10728-31

—— FOREIGN AID AS IT AFFECTS EMPLOYMENT IN THE UNITED STATES: Hon. Lawrence H. Smith, *Wisc.* Table of jobs affected, by States. Aug. 6, 1957; A6378-9

—— SO-CALLED MUTUAL SECURITY—THE DISTRIBUTION OF THE AMERICAN TAXPAYERS' WEALTH THROUGHOUT THE WORLD THROUGH INFLATION, FREE TRADE, AND CASH—PATTERN OF INTERNATIONAL SOCIALISM: Hon. George W. Malone, *Nev.* A 40-page presentation of foreign policy, aid and statistics (including tables) described on the Senate floor as "one of the greatest speeches I have ever heard made by any American." Aug 13, 1957; 13287-327

—— Debts of all nations, in current dollars. Aug. 13, 1957; 13291

—— Foreign grants and credits; TABLE 1: by program; TABLE 2: Military and other, by major country, July 1, 1945-Mar. 31, 1957. Aug. 13, 1957; 13316-26

—— MUTUAL SECURITY APPROPRIATIONS, 1958: Hon. William E. Jenner, *Ind.,* and other Senators. Impact of funds, with special reference to raw materials and the Western Hemisphere. Aug. 27, 1957; 14630 *e.s.*

—— COUNTERPART FUNDS. $2,510,700,000 used by six foreign nations (Austria, Denmark, France, Netherlands, Norway and United Kingdom) to reduce their national debts. Aug. 29, 1957; A7245

Tariff Commis- sion | THE TARIFF COMMISSION: Hon. Henderson L. Lanham, *Ga.* Its recommendations consistently ignored by the executive (documented); in effect, foreign political authorities are writing our tariff laws. (Includes statement of O. R. Strackbein, chairman of the Nationwide Committee of Industry, Agriculture and Labor on Import-Export Policy) Apr. 2, 1957; p. A2641

Memorials to Congress (for the preservation of America's economy)

State Legislatures — May 4, 1955. *California*, p. 4742; *Idaho*, p. 4741; *Nevada*, p. 4740; *Utah*, p. 4743 (See also Mar. 10, 1955; pp. 2164-5)

—— Mar. 4, 1957. *Nevada*, pp. 4517-8; *Idaho*, pp. 4519-20; *Alaska*, p. 4518

—— Mar. 28, 1957. *Pennsylvania*, pp. A2535-6

—— Apr. 17, 1957. *North Dakota*, p. A3045

—— Apr. 29, 1957. *Maine*, p. 5432

—— Apr. 30, 1957. *North Carolina*, p. A3205 (*re* grants-in-aid)

—— May 13, 1957. *Oklahoma*, p. 6011; *Vermont*, p. 6014

—— May 16, 1957. *New Hampshire*, p. 6291 (*re* grants-in-aid. This State "feels that its citizens know better than the Federal Government how to spend the citizens' money ... ")

—— May 27, 1957. *Florida*, p. 6827 (This memorial is *against* restricting imports of foreign crude oils)

—— June 3, 1957. *California*, p. 7289

—— June 10, 1957. *California*, on the Status of Forces agreement; p. 7643

—— . *Florida* proposes that sources of taxation be made available to the States, " . . . thereby enabling the States to finance their own traditional functions and thus eliminate Federal aid and control, reestablish State sovereignty, and eliminate the threat of possible despotic, inefficient, and chaotic centralization of government at the national level; . . . "; p. 7644

—— June 17, 1957. *Massachusetts*, on the Status of Forces agreement; p. 8278

—— . *South Carolina*, on the Status of Forces agreement; p. 8279

—— June 18, 1957. *California*, in regard to its fig industry; p. 8441

—— June 20, 1957. *Nebraska*, to modify the Status of Forces agreement; p. 8801

—— June 24, 1957. *Wisconsin*, in regard to plywood; p. 9029

—— July 2, 1957. *Vermont*, on the Status of Forces agreement; p. 9696

—— . *Illinois*, on the Status of Forces agreement; p. 9768

Western Governors' Conference — May 8, 1957; p. 5769. Resolution urging steps to prevent foreign dumping of cheaply produced minerals.

Western States' Conference — May 15, 1957; p. 6234. Republican Regional Conference of ten western States: Resolution to terminate the Trade Agreements Act when it expires in June 1958.

Municipali-   May 20, 1957; pp. 6411-2. City of Lowell, Mass.: Memorial on
ties   behalf of "the entire population of the city", calling for steps
              "in halting this menace to our industrial life".

———   May 27, 1957; p. A4077. City of Ft. Smith, Ark., urges passage
              of *H.R. 2815* (85/1), the General Imports Quota Act.

Labor, and   Feb. 28, 1957; p. 2449. Memorial from the crew of the *S. S.*
Labor   *Louisiana* (The Texas Co.), against legislation which will "take
Unions   our jobs from us, to be given over to cheap labor from foreign
              countries" . . . and to "do all in your power to help us now,
              and keep American cargoes in American ships, manned by
              American seamen."

———   May 2, 1957; p. A3316. Local 1651, United Steelworkers of
              America, AFL-CIO (Parkersburg, W. Va.) protest the importa-
              tion of cheap foreign shovels.

———   May 8, 1957; pp. A3486-7. Seafarers International Union of
              North America, AFL-CIO, at its Biennial Convention, "strongly
              oppose" joining the OTC, etc.

———   ILLINOIS LABOR SUGGESTS REVIEW OF OUR FOREIGN POLICY. Hon.
              Timothy P. Sheehan, *Ill.*, inserts (Oct. 1956) Statement of the
              Illinois State Federation of Labor. June 13, 1957; A4643

———   American Flint Glass Workers Union. Resolution favors adop-
              tion of the (Lanham) Import Quota Bill (*H. R. 2815,* 85/1)
              and opposes American entry into the OTC. July 12, 1957;
              A5589-90

———   International Brotherhood of Operative Potters, AFL-CIO. Reso-
              lution protests membership in OTC. Aug. 7, 1957; A6410-1

Proposals for Rectifying the Situation

(Selected, without prejudice, from the many advanced)

S. 28, 85/1   A BILL TO AMEND THE TARIFF ACT OF 1930. Introduced by
              Senator Malone on Jan. 7, 1957. To return to Congress the regu-
              lation of foreign trade, via the Tariff Commission, and to pro-
              vide for flexible duties. Apr. 16, 1957; 5171

S. 1723,   Senator Malone's bill to provide fair and reasonable competition
84/1   in imports, and for a flexible duty on them. Proposes restoration
              of the Tariff Commission to its former status, and a return to
              the Constitutional mandates in regard to trade. Apr. 18, 1955;
              pp. 3873-5

H.R. 1,   Amendment to *H.R. 1.* Proposed by Senator Malone. May 4,
84/1   1955; pp. 4734-60

Repeal of   REPEAL THE TRADE AGREEMENTS ACT AND RETURN TO THE CON-
the Original STITUTION OF THE UNITED STATES: Hon. George W. Malone.
Legislation   Jan. 12, 1956; pp. 351-62

H.R. 5102,   Introduced by Hon. Cleveland M. Bailey, *W. Va.* Designed not
85/1   simply to remedy, but to prevent, foreign dumping on America's
              markets. May 8, 1957; pp. 5925-6

S. 34, 85/1   Introduced by Senator Malone to provide a flexible tariff and to protect, *inter alia*, the strategic position of the U.S.A. in regard to its critical materials. June 24, 1957; 9056-8

S. 2375 and *S. 2376, 85/1*   IMPLEMENTATION OF LONG-RANGE MINERALS POLICY: Hon. Arthur V. Watkins, *Utah*. To alleviate mining industry's situation; detailed presentation of the status of specified critical materials. June 24, 1957; 9085-90

————   Proposal to amend the Trade Agreements Act and to provide for foreign wage-differentials. Hon. Thomas B. Curtis, *Mo.* Aug. 15, 1957; A6699-701

————   GENERAL IMPORT QUOTA BILL: Hon. Cleveland M. Bailey, *W. Va.* The executive departments' written position indicates their belief that "neither the Congress nor the Tariff Commission is to be entrusted with" the international or the domestic aspects of trade. July 11, 1957; 10297-300

H.J.R. 16 85/1   Introduced by Hon. Frank T. Bow, *Ohio,* to put an end to the Status of Forces agreements. Colorado editorial included. June 24, 1957; A5019

S. 2761 85/1   Introduced by Hon. Roman L. Hruska, *Nebr.,* to amend the Status of Forces agreements. Aug. 12, 1957; 13070-1

Quota Act   SELF-LIBERALIZING QUOTA BILL. Introduced by Hon. James T. Patterson, *Conn.* Discussion of the Bill, together with figures on imports of copper mill products. May 9, 1957; pp. A3569-72

————   The State Department's reply, in full, to proposed General Import Quota Bills (*H.R. 2566* and *H.R. 2776, 85/1*); reasons stated for its opposition to the Bills' passage. June 3, 1957; pp. 7383-8

Many of these and other references are available from Members of Congress upon request. Senator Malone has reprinted a great deal of usable data (not at Government expense). Reprints in quantity can often be had at very nominal cost.

(d) Documents of International Agencies and Agreements

"BUY AMERICAN" ACT. Repeal recommended by the Paley Commission. (The Paley Report, Vol. 1, pp. 79 and 164. June 1952)

———— *International Financial News Survey.* International Monetary Fund (IMF), 1818 H St., NW, Washington, D. C. Vol. VII; p. 11. Jan. 1954

———— Department of the Interior liberalizes its provisions. (Same ref: Vol. VIII, p. 171. Nov. 18, 1955)

GATT. *Basic Instruments and Selected Documents.*

VOL. I: Text of the [GATT] Agreements and Other Instruments and Procedures. Geneva, May 1952. 139 pp

VOL. II: Decisions, Declarations, Resolutions, Rulings and Reports. Geneva, May 1952. 228 pp

FIRST SUPPLEMENT: Contains decisions, declarations, resolutions and rulings; and reports of "working parties" of GATT. Geneva, Mar. 1953. 109 pp

SECOND SUPPLEMENT: Contains decisions, resolutions, etc.; reports adopted; and lists of documents. Geneva, Jan. 1954. 121 pp

VOL. I (revised): Contains text of GATT as it will be after amendment; the Agreement on the OTC drawn up at the ninth session of GATT. Geneva, Apr. 1955. 84 pp

THIRD SUPPLEMENT: Decisions, resolutions, reports, etc., of the ninth session of GATT. Geneva, June 1955. 296 pp

FOURTH SUPPLEMENT: Decisions, reports, etc., of the tenth session of GATT. Geneva, Feb. 1956. 141 pp. (This volume, pp. 96-9, contains GATT's Report *L/464*, Dec. 1, 1955, which report concerns GATT's examination of the First Annual Report submitted by the U. S. Government concerning measures taken by the U. S. Government in regard to its commitments on agricultural products. The report is of special concern to anyone engaged in dairy products, cotton, wheat and wheat flour. It recommends, for instance, that the Netherlands restrict the import of American wheat flour to 60,000 metric tons during 1956 in view of our non-relaxation of restrictions on Dutch dairy products pursuant to GATT's resolution of Nov. 5, 1954)

—— *Waiver Granted to the United States in Connection with Import Restrictions Imposed under Section 22 of the United States Agricultural Adjustment Act (of 1933), as Amended.* Decision of Mar. 5, 1955

———— *Congressional Record,* May 4, 1955; p. 4747

———— Press Release *GATT/258.* United Nations. Geneva, Nov. 28, 1955

—— SWITZERLAND AND GATT. UN Press Release *GATT/314.* Geneva, Oct. 26, 1956 (Also *The Journal of Commerce,* New York, Nov. 19, 1956

GATT AND THE IMF. Statement of Irving S. Friedman, Director of Exchange Restrictions Department of the IMF, before the Subcommittee on Foreign Economic Policy of the Joint Committee on the Economic Report, Nov. 14, 1955. Also reported in *International Financial News Survey* (Vol. VII, No. 22; Nov. 25, 1955). International Monetary Fund, Washington, D. C.

EUROPEAN RECOVERY, STERLING ATTITUDE, DOLLAR GAP, U. S. INVESTMENTS ABROAD. Address of Viscount Harcourt, Economic Minister, British Embassy, Washington, D. C. Executive Director of the IMF, for the United Kingdom. Harcourt's address before the Investment Bankers' Assn. in New York (Oct. 19, 1955) is reported in *Financial News Survey* (Vol. VIII, No. 18; Oct. 28, 1955). Int'l. Monetary Fund, Washington, D. C.

ECONOMIC DEVELOPMENT INSTITUTE. Address by Eugene R. Black, president of the International Bank, Sept. 12, 1955. The EDI has been established "with financial assistance from the Ford and Rockefeller Foundations." *Financial News Survey* (Vol. VIII, No. 13; Sept. 23, 1955). IMF, Washington, D. C.

INTERNATIONAL FINANCE CORPORATION. List of signatories to date, and proposed subscriptions and participants. Int'l. Bank for Reconstruction and Development, *Press Release.* Washington, D. C. Nov. 25, 1955

Other References

COTTON. 1955 crop estimated at 14.8 million bales; surplus total, 10.6 million bales. *The Wall Street Journal*, New York. Nov. 9, 1955

———— USDA offers cotton at 6c-8c below domestic market price. *Idem*. Feb. 29, 1956

———— FOREIGN COUNTRIES PROTEST U. S. COTTON EXPORT POLICY. *The Washington Post and Times-Herald*. Washington, D. C. Mar. 6, 1956

———— REVIEW OF THE WORLD SITUATION. *Cotton*. Int'l. Cotton Advisory Committee, South Agricultural Bldg., Washington, D. C. Vol. 9, Nos. 9, 10; Apr.-May 1956

———— COTTON TEXTILES SUBSIDIZED. *The Wall Street Journal*, New York. May 22, 1956

———— SUBSIDIES CAUSING THE SURPLUS. Lewis Haney, syndicated column. *New York Journal-American*, May 23, 1956

———— Address of Roger Fleming, Sec.-Treas., American Farm Bureau Federation. *The National Program Letter*. Harding College, Searcy, Ark. Sept. 1956

———— Exports estimated at 6 million bales for year ending July 31, 1957. *The Wall Street Journal*, New York. Nov. 5, 1956

———— "Soil Bank" program to reduce cotton acreage 25% in 1957. *The Cotton Situation*. Dept. of Agriculture, Washington, D. C. Feb. 5, 1957

WHEAT. REASONS FOR SURPLUS. Henry J. Taylor, nationwide broadcast. Feb. 20, 1956

———— Sales to West Germany. *Neue Zürcher Zeitung*, Zurich. May 8, 1956

———— ICA to sell cotton and wheat to France. CCC barter transactions. *The Journal of Commerce*, New York. Aug. 30, 1956

TOBACCO. OUR FOURTH LARGEST CROP. Henry J. Taylor, nationwide broadcast. Mar 5, 1956

———— The United Kingdom purchases American tobacco, continues to limit its import. *The Times*, London. June 9, 1956

WOOL. Surplus sales. *The Wall Street Journal*, New York. Sept. 9, 1955

———— Tariff quota imposed on wool fabrics. *Idem*, Oct. 1, 1956

DRIED MILK. Surplus sales. *Idem*, Sept. 9, 1956

GENERAL. LOSSES ON THE SUPPORT PROGRAM. *The Journal of Commerce*, New York. Sept. 22, 1955. (Losses $800,000,000 during fiscal 1955)

———— Government holdings of farm products. *The Wall Street Journal*, New York. Dec. 6, 1955

———— Sales and barter agreements with France, Germany and Viet-Nam. *Neue Zürcher Zeitung*, Zurich. May 8, 1956. *L'Information de Viet-Nam Economique et Financière*, Saigon, Viet-Nam. May 10, 1956

———— Viet-Nam celebrates *Tet. Idem*. Aug. 16, 1956; also, *Marchés Coloniaux du Monde*, Paris. Aug. 25, 1956

———— Agreement with India, the receipts in rupees, for the sale of 200,000 tons of surplus rice. *The Hindu Weekly Review*, Madras, India. Jan. 14, 1957

———— Agreement with Burma, counterpart funds in kyats, for $17,300,000.

In addition, a $25,000,000 loan to Burma from the ICA. ICA *Press Release*, Mar. 21, 1957

—— Agreement with Austria, totalling $24,700,000. The counterpart funds, in schillings, to be used by Austria. *Austrian Information*. Austrian Information Service, New York. May 25, 1957

—— Agreement with Poland to sell surplus products for zlotys. Dept. of State *Press Release*, June 7, 1957. Total amount in agreement, $95,000,-000.

SHIPPING. *The Log*, particularly Vol. 50, No. 9. Aug. 31, 1955. Further references: EISENHOWER SIGNS 50-50 CARGO BILL (Sept. 1954); FOREIGN OPERATORS BLAST THE 50-50 LAW (June 1955); WHO WROTE THE DEATH SENTENCE FOR 50-50 BILL, and EFFRONTERY AND CONSUMMATE GALL (FOREIGN SHIPPING LOBBY) (July 1955). *The Log* is now incorporated in *Marine Engineering*, Simmons-Boardman Publishing Corp., 30 Church St., New York 7, N. Y.

—— Reports of the American Merchant Marine Institute.

—— SHIP CONSTRUCTION IN PRIVATE U. S. SHIPYARDS, 1914-54. Tabulated by class, tonnage and number of ships. TABLES AND CHARTS Nos. 23, 24. Shipbuilders Council of America, 21 West St., New York 6, N. Y.

—— The Japanese launch a tanker for American interests. *Life*, Aug. 29, 1955; pp. 47-8

LINEN TOWELS. To compensate for lowered duty, U. S. agrees to reduce levy on six commodities. *Foreign Commerce Weekly*, Dept. of Commerce. July 8, 1957

MACHINERY. Manufacturers of heavy electrical equipment appeal to Government to bar federal purchases of foreign-made hydraulic turbines. Appeal denied. *The Journal of Commerce*, New York. Mar. 15, 1957

FLUORSPAR. *The Wall Street Journal*, New York. Sept. 9, 1955

—— President rejects recommendation of Tariff Commission for duty increase. *The Journal of Commerce*, New York. Mar 21, 1956

FISH. Increased duty on groundfish denied. *Idem*, Dec. 11, 1956

BRITAIN. Percentages of "American" products in Britain; foreign restrictions against U. S. products. *District Bank Review*, Manchester, England. Sept. 1955

—— Wage scales in Britain. *Industrial News*, No. 19. Oct. 14, 1955. Trades Union Congress, Smith Square, London SW 1

CANADA. CANADA'S AMERICAN BOOM: R. A. Farquharson, Counsellor of the Canadian Embassy at Washington, D. C. *Vital Speeches of the Day*, New York, Sept. 1, 1957

GROSS NATIONAL PRODUCT. Henry J. Taylor, nationwide broadcast. Oct. 1, 1956

—— Annual rate reaches $413.8 billion during 3d quarter of 1956. *The Journal of Commerce*, New York. Nov. 13, 1956

—— Inflation reaches $83,000,000,000 in terms of the 1947 dollar. *Money-Matters*, Aug. 1957. Institute of Life Insurance, 488 Madison Ave., New York 22. (Source of the figure: Dept. of Commerce)

PRIVATE INVESTMENT ABROAD. Increment during 1955, and present total. Dept. of Commerce *Press Release*, Aug. 20, 1955

"Dollar-gap". *Business in Brief* (quarterly). Chase Manhattan Bank, New York. Oct. 1955

Defense Department. Assets and employed personnel. Henry J. Taylor, nationwide broadcast. Oct. 10, 1955

Executive Agencies—Employment Figures, 1957. UP despatch, Sept. 4, 1957. *Daily News,* New York, Sept. 5; p. 28. Paul O. Peters, *News Bulletin* No. 172 (1957); 939 D St., Washington 4, D. C.: Study of the Growth and Cost of the Federal Bureaucracy: 1930 to 1956. June 8, 1956

Strategic Materials. The Proof. Editorial commending *Senate Report 1627,* 83/2. *Post-Intelligencer,* Seattle, Wash. Jan. 31, 1955

GATT. Foreign diplomat says the U. S. is "flagrantly breaking the spirit of GATT." National City Bank *Letter,* New York. June, 1955

—— Concessions under GATT. *The Journal of Commerce,* New York. June 8, 1956

Transoceanic Development Corporation organized. *Idem,* Oct. 4, 1955

Foreign Aid. Let's Be Sensible About Foreign Aid: Clarence B. Randall. The views of one businessman in Government. *Saturday Evening Post,* June 22, 1957

Tariffs. National Planning Association program for broad slashing of tariffs. Includes a program for Government aid in moving workers to areas where new employment would be available. Compiled by Dr. D. Humphrey, Duke University economist. Published by the Twentieth Century Fund, New York. 1956. 564 pp ($6.00)

Debt Changes in 1956. Dept. of Commerce, Office of Business Economics. Washington, D.C. May 28, 1957

Books

All New Wealth Comes from the Soil: Carl H. Wilken. Raw Materials National Council, 1613 35th St., N. W., Washington, D. C. 1957 ($1.25)

Corporate Profits in the Decade 1947-56: George Terborgh. Machinery & Allied Products Institute, 1200 18th St., N. W., Washington, D. C. Aug. 1957 ($1.25)

A Charter for the Social Sciences in the Schools (Report of the Commission on the Social Studies: Part I): Charles A. Beard. Charles Scribner's Sons. New York. 1932

Government by Treason: John Howland Snow. The Long House, Inc. New York. 1946 ($1.00)

The Vision and the Constant Star: A. H. Hobbs. The Long House, Inc. New York. 1956 ($3.50)

The Turning of the Tides: Hon. Paul W. Shafer and John Howland Snow. The Long House, Inc., New York, 1953, 1956 (Paperbound, fully sewn, $2.00; Library Edition, $3.00)

INDEX OF PRODUCTS AND INDUSTRIES

Further data, highly pertinent, will be found in the Classified Bibliography *under their appropriate headings.*

GENERAL INDEX

123

CPSIA information can be obtained
at www.ICGtesting.com
Printed in the USA
LVHW081034271218
601183LV00040B/922/P